BK 746.4 G884H
HISTORY OF NEEDLEWORK TOOLS AND ACCESSORIES
/GROVES, SY
1973 10.00 FV

3000 435816 30019

St. Louis Community College

746.4 G884h EV

GROVES

THE HISTORY OF NEEDLEWORK
TOOLS AND ACCESSORIES

10.00

S0-AHD-891

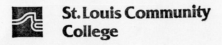
WITHDRAWN

St. Louis Community College

Library

5801 Wilson Avenue
St. Louis, Missouri 63110

THE HISTORY OF
Needlework Tools
AND ACCESSORIES

THE HISTORY OF

Needlework Tools

AND ACCESSORIES

SYLVIA GROVES

ARCO PUBLISHING COMPANY, INC
NEW YORK

Library of Congress Catalog Card Number 72-97034

ISBN 0-668-02953-6

Published 1973 by Arco Publishing
Company, Inc.
219 Park Avenue South, New York,
N.Y. 10003

© Sylvia Groves 1966, 1968, 1973
All rights reserved

Printed in Great Britain

Contents

THE PRAYSE OF THE NEEDLE

To all dispersed sorts of Arts and Trades,
I writ the Needle's prayse (that never fades).
So long as children shall be got or borne,
So long as garments shall be made or worne,
So long as Hemp or Flax, or Sheep shall bear
Their linnen wollen fleeces yeare by yeare,
So long as Silk-wormes, with exhausted spoile,
Of their owne Entrailes for man's gaine shall toyle,
Yea till the world be quite dissolv'd and past,
So long at least, the Needle's use shall last.

From *The Prayse of the Needle* by
John Taylor, the 'water-poet' (1580–1653).

Illustrations

Objects illustrated are from the author's own collection unless otherwise indicated.

HALF-TONE PLATES

Illustrations

Illustrations

LINE DRAWINGS IN THE TEXT

Acknowledgments

I should like first to express my most grateful thanks to Mr Charles Thomas, who is responsible for the drawings and for all the illustrations of tools and needlework in my own collection, in particular for his patience and skill in arranging, balancing and photographing numerous small objects in a wide variety of materials, more exacting in their requirements as to lighting and background than any *prima-donna*. To Mrs Penelope Collins I should like to express my gratitude for the loan of tools, notes and other material, and for her generous co-operation in many side-lines of research.

My thanks are also due to those authorities and individuals who have allowed objects in their possession to be photographed, or have permitted the reproduction of copyright photographs; their names will be found in the list of illustrations.

Plates 138 and 184 are reproduced by permission of the Trustees of the Wallace Collection, and Plate 146 by courtesy of the Trustees of the National Gallery.

Especial mention must also be made of the generous help given to me by Mr Paul Bernheimer, Cambridge, Mass.; Mr Ross Newhouse of Newhouse Galleries, New York; Israel Sack Inc., New York; Mr John Herbert of Christies; Messrs Knoedler and Co.; Mr H. M. Lee of Chichester Antiques; The London Museum; Brighton Art Gallery and Museum; The Castle Museum, Norwich; Sheffield City Museum; The Trustees of the Lady Lever Art Gallery, Port Sunlight; Le Musée Fabre, Montpellier; and the Walters Art Gallery, Baltimore.

To Mr G. Bernard Mason, and Mr and Mrs Edward Pinto, I am grateful not only for photographs, but for much information regarding objects in their collections, and for their kind encouragement over a number of years; to Mrs Zoe Watkin for the detailed description of her work-boxes and to Miss Angela Watkin for photographing them; to the Embroiderers' Guild for the loan of needlework and of books from their very extensive library; and to Mr C. E. Freeman of Luton Museum for assisting in the identification of lace-bobbins.

Others to whom I should like to express my gratitude for their help in many different ways are: Miss V. M. Walker of Nottingham Public Libraries; Redditch Public Library; Mr H. Westwood of the Birmingham Assay Office; Mrs O. Feigl; Mrs T. Downing; Miss J. A. Thomas; Prof. and Mrs J. H.

Whitfield; Mrs H. Challenor; Mrs A. Stephens; Miss S. Littlejohn; Miss S. Mathew and Mr and Mrs G. Hake.

In conclusion, I should like to acknowledge my indebtedness to the staff of the Birmingham Library, Margaret Street, who have so willingly descended into basements and climbed to the tops of ladders in search of little-read and inaccessible books, and to Mrs E. M. Forster for her help and advice in the preparation of the manuscript in its final stages.

Foreword

A rich legacy from the past, in national and other collections, offers ample opportunity for the detailed study of the stitching and embroidery of former centuries, and places a wealth of material at the disposal of writers who specialise in the various branches of these subjects. For an author setting out to write a book on needlework implements or tools there is no such background of well-documented evidence. The voyage of discovery on which I had embarked, as I was soon to learn, was to a largely uncharted country, the extent and depth of which did not become apparent until I was well on my way. Sources referred to are mentioned in the text or footnotes, but books dealing directly with the subject are too few to warrant a bibliography.

The history of needlework implements is, of course, linked inseparably with the history of needlework itself. As the skill of the craftsman, developing slowly through the centuries, enabled him to produce implements of a gradually increasing delicacy, so, in a like manner, the inventiveness of the needlewoman in exploring new and more elaborate techniques called for tools of an even greater fineness. Changing social customs and the dictates of fashion brought, in their turn, a demand for accessories in endless variety. To emphasise the importance of a tool, therefore, or to explain the background against which it emerged, I have included among the illustrations some examples of the work of the type or period concerned—merely to describe an implement or to define its purpose would be, in many instances, to tell but half its story. My intention, moreover, has been not simply to trace the bare history of needlework tools, but to help collectors, students and all who may be interested in needlework itself to recognise and date various forms of work through a better understanding of the implements and of the processes involved, and of the needs and customs that have played so important a part in their development.

Edgbaston   SYLVIA GROVES

Needles and Needle-cases

SEWING NEEDLES are such necessary articles of everyday use that they have been made from the earliest times by people of all races. They have been fashioned from thorns and fish bones, carved from wood, bone, ivory and shell, and hammered out of a variety of metals, including gold and silver. In the early stone age when sewing was confined to the stitching together of tough hides, a sharp awl, probably of flint, was used for piercing the skins, and a thread of sinew, attached to a thorn or slender bone, passed through the ready-made holes. In course of time, the invention of woven cloth made it possible to combine these two operations, and a needle having an eye at one end came into use, a spun thread taking the place of the sinew.

Improvements in the technique of weaving and of stitchery were necessarily slow, but it is obvious that the diaphanous and delicately embroidered fabrics depicted in the art of ancient Egypt, Greece and Italy must have demanded implements of extreme fineness, not unlike those of the present day, a demand which the supreme skill of the craftsmen of these countries would have had little difficulty in satisfying. The extent to which steel needles were available to the ancient civilisations of the West is impossible to determine owing to the fact that no fine needle made of steel could have escaped the destructive action of rust. On the other hand, those of bronze, a metal much more resistant to corrosion, have survived in some quantity. From their general crudeness, however, and the thickness of the eye which, in the repeated piercing of the cloth, would have damaged any fine fabric, it is evident that very many of them were never intended for domestic sewing as we understand the term today (Fig. 1). The explanation of this is that they were needed for a form of needlework now almost forgotten, namely, the sewing up of all kinds of packages in an outer covering of cloth or leather for the purpose of storage or transport. The importance of this operation, even up to the 19th century, may be estimated by the number of words such as packing-needle, pack-thread, pack-cloth or pack-sheet (a coarse cloth woven specially for packing goods) which still survive in our dictionaries; and it is also significant that what is probably the earliest reference to a needle in English literature, in Langland's *Piers the Plowman*, is to a 'paknedel'.

Until the Tudor period at least, the bronze needles used in England were made by individual craftsmen in various parts of the country. One of the patrons of the Inn that Langland describes in his poem is 'Hughe the nedeler'. The technique employed by the needler of this era was simple and effective. A piece of bronze wire was cut to the length of a needle and the eye end flattened on an anvil with a small hammer. The eye itself was made by striking into the flattened part with a punch on the anvil, and clearing the hole with a sharper punch on a cake of lead. The wire was then held securely in grooved

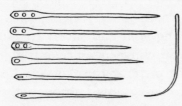

Fig. 1. Ancient Roman bronze needles, some with multiple eyes to prevent the thread slipping.

pliers and rested against a wooden block fixed in a bench while the point was formed, and the head trimmed and smoothed, with files. Finally, with a guttering iron, a groove was filed down the eye, on both sides, to accommodate some of the thickness of the thread.

The needler sold most of his small stock to the hucksters, who set up their booths at the markets and fairs of neighbouring towns, and to the pedlars who, with their heavy packs, tramped many a mile along dusty roads and rough grass tracks to the doors of scattered cottages and country mansions alike. In the winter these roads were often impassable. For people living in the remoter districts a visit to the nearest town, or the arrival of the packman, might be long delayed. The possession of a good needle was thus a matter of great importance as, if broken or mislaid, its loss could not always be made good. The plot of the 16th-century comedy *Gammer Gurton's Needle*, revolving round just such a predicament, was readily appreciated by the audiences of the times; while to the social historian of today it is of interest that Gammer Gurton, who kept several servants and was in a position to command the attentions of the village parson and the doctor, possessed only one needle, the loss of which was a major disaster in her household.

To guard against a catastrophe of this kind some medieval needles were provided with a slight kink halfway between the point and the eye, at right angles to the eye opening (Plate 1). This did not hinder the movement of the needle appreciably when in use, but prevented it from slipping out if left in the material when the work was laid aside. What was equally important was that the needle could not fall out of the open-ended needle-cases, which were, at this period, worn hanging from the waist. These needle-cases, in their simplest form, consisted of a short length of bone or wood, carved, perhaps, with some simple design, and hollowed out so that it would move freely up and down when threaded on to a length of cord. The cord was attached at one end to the girdle, while at the other end was sewn a piece of material into which one or two needles could be stuck. When not in use the needles were covered by the tubular case, which was drawn down over them; when a needle was required, the case was pushed upward, leaving the material exposed. A ring, sewn to the lower end of the material, prevented the tube from sliding off when the needles were covered.

A particularly interesting case of this kind, of early 16th-century date, cast in bronze in the form of a fish, is shown in Plate 1. In this instance a length of fine cord attached to the upper end of the material is looped through a hole in a projection on the underside of the fish's mouth. To expose a needle, this cord is loosened with one hand and the case drawn upward with the other.

Among the hanging needle-cases worn by ladies in the highest ranks of society in the Middle Ages there were exquisite examples of the goldsmith's art. These cases were flat, but functioned in exactly the same way as those of tubular form; they were usually lozenge shaped,[1] thus providing a suitable surface for the setting of gem stones and for other rich decoration (Plate 2). Very few of them now exist owing to the practice, prevalent in those times, of sending outmoded jewellery and silverwork back to the craftsmen, to be broken up and re-worked into objects in the prevailing taste; the very fact of their richness militated against the possibility of their survival in any but the most exceptional circumstances.

In Tudor England the lozenge gave way to a rectangular form, but, as the bronze needle was soon to be replaced by the finer, steel needle, calling for a different method of storage, the open-ended needle-case passed out of fashion. In some countries, however, it still survived; a tubular case from Lapland, of more recent date, is shown in Plate 3; it is made almost entirely from the bone and skin of the reindeer, only a small fragment of scarlet woollen cloth being inserted. The needle, which is of steel, is threaded with a fine reindeer sinew, and has a triangular point for piercing leather.

We owe some knowledge of the introduction of the steel needle into England to John Stow, who published his famous *Survey of London and Westminster* in 1598. Stow was a tailor in his younger days, which would account

[1] See British Museum *Guide to Mediaeval Antiquities*, 1924.

for his interest in the subject. To him a steel needle was a 'Spanish needle'. Originating in China some centuries B.C., the manufacture of needles from steel had reached the Near East at an early date, and from Damascus, long famous for its work in steel, was carried by the Moors into Spain, where, during the Middle Ages, Cordoba became a great needle-making centre. Katherine of Aragon, who arrived here with her train in the opening years of the 16th century and became renowned for her interest in needlework, no doubt brought with her a supply of steel needles from her native land. When contacts between this country and Spain were further strengthened by the marriage of Katherine's daughter, Mary, with her cousin, Philip of Spain, it may be assumed with some confidence that no lady at the English court would have lacked a smooth steel needle for her embroidery. With regard to their manufacture in this country, Stow records that: 'In Mary's time there was a negro made fine steel needles in Cheapside, but would never teach his art to any.' The Negro referred to was undoubtedly a Spanish Moor. Stow further relates that 'the making of Spanish needles was first taught in England by Elias Crowse (or Krause) a German, about the 8th year of Queen Elizabeth'. Crowse was probably a native of Nuremberg, a town that had been a centre of the steel needle trade as early as the 14th century.

It must, however, be remembered that the information provided by Stow was derived from his own experiences in the City of London, and that, with the limited communication of the times, he may have been unaware of developments in other parts of the country. In the archives of the Quirinal, in Rome, there is a record to the effect that needle making was one of the industries practised in English monasteries before the Reformation. 'What man', complained John Wycliffe, 'is so busie about marchandise, and other worldly doings, as bene Preists.' On the other hand, one might ask, who were better qualified than the monks and friars, in those days of general poverty and ignorance, to organise these industries in which lay brothers and numerous other workers found useful employment? It is certainly no mere coincidence that a derelict steel needle mill still stands on the site of Bordesley Abbey, near Redditch in Worcestershire.

In London, the needlemakers established their shops near the tailors and drapers in Cheapside and Threeneedle Street, so called from the three needles on the Shield of Arms of the Worshipful Company of Needlemakers and now corrupted to Threadneedle Street, and also in nearby Whitechapel. The presence of alien needlemakers in the City was evidently resented for, in the early 1600s, the Company, as the result of a petition, forbade their use of 'engines', probably the drop-stamp, which it was claimed produced inferior work, was dangerous to the workers and deprived many of their means of livelihood. The policy was a mistaken one for, as a consequence, needlemakers gradually moved out of the capital to localities where they could escape such irksome restrictions. In 1650 some are known to have settled and prospered at Long Crendon in Buckinghamshire; but the general exodus did not take place until the 18th century, when the problem of obtaining water power caused them to spread to other parts of the country and brought them, ultimately, into contact with fellow workers at Redditch, where steel needle making was already a flourishing industry. At the end of the 18th century the Rev. T. R. Nash, in his *History of Worcestershire*, stated that at that time there were about 400 people employed in needle manufacture at Redditch. Today, of course, Redditch needles are known throughout the world.

The problems facing the makers of steel needles were very different from those of their predecessors who had worked in bronze. They not only had to acquire a practical knowledge of the heat treatment of steel in annealing, hardening and tempering, but technical developments were turning them into skilled toolmakers and mechanics. The small country workshops of earlier times could not hope to compete with the well-organised centres of manu-facture where steel needles were being produced in ever-increasing quantities, while improved means of transport were simplifying the task of distribution.

It is no easy matter to select steel needles which can be used to illustrate the development in the processes of their manufacture. Since John Stow first considered them worthy of mention, they have been regarded as articles for immediate use rather than for careful preservation for the benefit of future generations. The two steel needles shown on the right of Plate 1 may, how-ever, be reasonably presumed, from their provenance, to date from about the year 1700. The smaller one is well made, perhaps by an Oriental needler who attached importance to good workmanship rather than to an economy of time; the larger, comparatively poor as to finish, displays advances in tech-nique which have remained fundamentally unchanged and have been brought to greater perfection in modern times.

The main stages in the actual making of steel needles are illustrated in Fig. 2. The methods employed were as follows: The steel wire was received at the needle-mill in coils, which were cut up into pieces equal to the length of two needles. To remove the curve a very ingenious method was employed: two iron rings, of about eight inches diameter, were placed on edge a short distance apart and packed nearly full of wires. The rings, with the wires, were then placed in a furnace and brought to a dull red heat, when they were transferred to a flat iron slab, where a curved iron bar, with slots to fit over the rings, was used to roll them backwards and forwards (Fig. 3); when taken out of the rings the wires were perfectly straight. After annealing, they were passed to the pointers who sat before large grindstones driven by water power. Each man arranged two dozen or more wires at a time across the palm of his hand and revolved them by a skilful backward and forward motion of

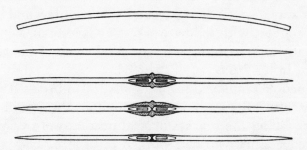

Fig. 2. The five main stages in the manufacture of a modern steel needle.

the thumb while pressing them against the stone. When both ends had been sharpened in this way, the wires were taken to the Stamping and Eyeing Shop. The illustration shown in Plate 4 is taken from a journal of the mid 19th century; but such a workshop had altered very little in its essential features over a long period. On the left are three drop-stamps; with a blow from these, the two eyes were formed at the centre of each piece of wire as it was struck between the dies mounted on the stamp. It was then necessary to anneal the wires again before proceeding.

Fig. 3. Device for straightening wires for making needles.

Eyeing consists in punching out the thin film of metal remaining in the eyes after stamping, the operation being performed by the girls seated at the screw presses. The twin needles were next threaded on two parallel wires, one through each of the eyes, to keep them in the same relative position. Packed tightly together, they were fixed between wooden clamps and screwed in a vice while the 'flash', the surplus metal forced out in stamping, was filed away. The two sets of needles were then broken apart and the tops of each set in turn smoothed off, before the wires were removed. After hardening and tempering, they were ready for polishing, or 'scouring' as it was termed, a highly specialised process.

For this purpose a large piece of stout cloth was spread out and needles to the number of a hundred thousand or more arranged upon it and sprinkled over with a fine abrasive and with a solution of soft soap as a lubricant; the cloth was then rolled up and the roll tied at each end and securely bound with cord. Several of these bundles were placed on a long bench with a heavy block of wood on top of them, and two men, one at each end of the bench, propelled the block backwards and forwards for about eighteen hours, rolling the bundles beneath. At a later period water supplied the necessary power for this operation. A scouring mill, worked by a water-wheel and said to have been used in the 17th century, is still standing near Redditch.

After scouring, the needles were removed from the cloth and washed clean with soap and water, and, after being bundled as before, the same process was repeated with a polishing powder, to give them the high finish which is characteristic of English needles; a final refinement was the polishing of the interior of the eye. During the 20th century, most of the hand operations have been replaced by mechanisation, but the processes remain fundamentally the same as those described above.

By Queen Anne's reign the supply of steel needles was comparatively plentiful. The open-ended needle-case had disappeared, and had been followed by its logical successor the needle-book. Lady Grizel Baillie, when on a tour of the Continent in 1733, bought several needle-books from a convent in Paris; these, no doubt, had embroidered covers worked by the nuns. For the storage of steel needles, however, needle-books did not prove entirely satisfactory as their flannel leaves attracted moisture from the atmosphere, thereby encouraging rust. Tightly closed cylindrical cases were, in general, found to be more suitable as containers. Some of the earliest of these took the form of small standing figures, carved from ivory, about three inches in height, and divided at the middle, the top screwing into the bottom (Plate 7). They were usually of Continental origin and represented peasants in their national costume. Many were carved in the form of fisher folk with a net or the day's catch in their hand, and were made in coastal districts near the European ports where they met with a ready sale among sailors and travellers, who bought them to take home to their families. In the latter part of the last century, one of these small figures might occasionally be seen standing on a cottage mantel-shelf, a relic of the days when a needle was still a domestic treasure and a needle-case a household rather than a personal possession.

With the Georgian era cylindrical needle-cases came into common use (Plates 5 and 6) They were fashioned from a great variety of materials and were often of the most delicate workmanship. Some were of carved ivory, mounted with gold; others were of tortoiseshell with piqué decoration and often with a cartouche for a monogram. French cases of *vernis Martin*, or ivory cases with small panels of *verre églomisé*, bore such sentiments as '*à l'amitié*' or '*point de partage en amour*'. From France also came multi-coloured beaded cases, the slender containers turned from bone, with the beads, threaded on fine wire, wound round them, each row attached to the next with silk stitching. Straw marquetry was yet another form of ornamentation used in France, and also in Italy, where small, flat cases with a sliding lid or drawer were carved from wood or ivory and decorated with steel studs (Plate 8).

For a woman of education in the 18th and early 19th centuries, skill in the art of letter writing was considered as important as proficiency in the use of the needle. It is not unusual therefore to find writing and sewing accessories combined. The standing needle-case in Plate 8, topped with a thimble, has a seal base and a small compartment for wafers; the ivory handle of the seal in Plate 6 unscrews from its base and is hollowed out to hold needles. In the same category, though less common, is the needle-case in Plate 9, where the lower part is made in the form of a perpetual calendar.

The majority of needle-cases are tubular, as they are turned and for the most part decorated, in a lathe. This treatment is not suited to all materials; the lustre of mother-of-pearl is visible only on the front and back of the shell and not at all on cross-sections. Pearl needle-cases are consequently more or less oblong in section, displaying two wide areas of luminous shell, with the sides as narrow as possible. Many of the more expensive ivory cases are of this section as the quality of the material is thus shown to advantage, and a larger area is provided for enrichment by gold inlay, *verre églomisé*, or enamel. Beadwork examples may take an elliptical form, while tortoiseshell cases moulded to this shape are usually decorated with piqué work (Plate 10). Fitted work-boxes often contain flat ivory cases carved as Cupid's quiver and arrows, sometimes with a decoration of steel piqué, or bearing amorous messages in *verre églomisé*.

It is by no means unusual in an old needle-case to find bodkins in place of, or as well as, needles. The difference between a needle-case and a bodkin-case is purely a matter of size (Plates 10 and 11), and until the end of the 18th century the use of the term was often arbitrary. But whereas a small case, designed only to hold a few sewing needles, was intended for feminine use, bodkin-cases were owned by men as well as women, for bodkins in earlier centuries were of equal importance to both sexes. They were needed for running in drawstrings and threading and re-threading ribbons, cords and laces with which so many garments were fastened. In 1652, Sir Ralph Verney, having been driven by his conscience to seek exile in France, wrote to his home in Buckinghamshire for his 'Black leather needlecase with great gold Bodkin, Paper of Pinns, Blew Thread Shirt Buttons and old White Round Buttons, Cap Strings and Tape'. The large bodkins of this period, seven or more inches long, sometimes terminated in an ear-spoon and were also engraved with initials and a date (Plate 13 and Fig. 5).

By the late 18th century silver bodkins, now comparatively small, were being made as presents and souvenirs and might be stamped with some simple phrase such as 'forget-me-not' (Plate 10). A bereavement in the Royal Family was commemorated in 1817 by the manufacture of bodkins bearing the name of Princess Charlotte and the date of her death. For the collector an even more uncommon find is a tortoiseshell or mother-of-pearl case containing a bodkin made from the same material. References to bodkins occasionally occur in old wills and inventories, but may be misleading, as in former centuries the term bodkin was applied to the dagger-like ornaments that women were accustomed to wear in their hair. Lady Mary Wortley Montagu, for instance, describing her visit to the Viennese Court in 1716, mentions the 'three or four rows of bodkins, wonderfully large,' sticking out two or three inches from the enormous head-dresses that were in fashion at this time. Stilettos, on account of their dagger-like appearance, might also be termed bodkins. Any early reference to these implements must therefore be read with care and interpreted according to the immediate context.

By the end of the 18th century the craft of needle making had reached such perfection that needles of extreme fineness (less than one-hundredth of an inch in diameter) had become readily available, enabling ladies of leisure to display their skill in needlework of a new type, namely Print Work. This was the reproduction of small engravings and etchings, using the finest black and grey threads or, very occasionally, human hair, on a background of white silk. In 1781 Sylas Neville, in his *Diary*, mentions having seen near Norwich 'a charming piece of needlework. It represents a view upon a lake near Berne, has all the appearance of the finest engraving, is done upon sarsanet with black silk. The stitches are minute to a degree.' An example of one such picture, which has the effect of an etching, is shown in Plate 12. The advent of the darning sampler at this period (Plate 17) was also connected with the production of very fine needles.

An invention of the 19th century was the calyx-eyed needle. Here, the blunt end, terminating in a V-shaped notch, was split, so that the thread, when pressed downward into the notch, could be sprung into the eye—a boon, it was claimed, to those with failing sight. Needles were now sold in numbered sizes wrapped in a special blue paper to prevent rusting. The cylindrical cases were being replaced by small, upright boxes resembling knife-boxes with sloping lids, accommodating packets of different lengths (Plate 14). In 1809 Elizabeth Grant of Rothiemurchus, in her *Memoirs of a Highland Lady*, recalls that Sir Robert Ainslie 'brought to my Mother the first of those little morocco cases full of needles she had ever seen, where the papers were all arranged in sizes, on a slope, which made it easy to select from them'. These boxes enjoyed a wide popularity until they, in their turn, were ousted by the more convenient needle-book which had returned to favour with the advent of the work-box (Plate 15).

It now became fashionable to make needle holders in the form of toys. An amusing variant of the needle-book was a roll-up case consisting of a strip of white silk painted with a row of soldiers, each having a needle for a bayonet. No less a poet than Wordsworth was inspired to write ten verses 'Composed on seeing a lady making a needle-case in the form of a harp', actually the work of Miss Southey, daughter of the Poet Laureate:

> *A very harp in all but size!*
> *Needles for strings in apt gradation.*
> *Minerva's self would stigmatize*
> *The unclassic profanation.*

Standing figure needle-cases carved from wood were also made in the 19th century, particularly in Austria and Switzerland, where they were bought by tourists. They may be distinguished from those of an earlier period by the fact that the figure is placed on a pedestal which is hollowed to hold the needles (Plate 14). Miniature umbrellas were made in considerable quantities and sold as souvenirs at popular resorts, the handles often containing a magnifying lens through which a series of minute photographic views could be seen.

Early in Queen Victoria's reign a few manufacturers, anxious to make their products more attractive, began, as an experiment, to sell their needles in small cardboard boxes decorated with a picture on the lid. The following advertisement, which appeared in 1845, is typical of this innovation:

'H. Walker's needles (by authority the "Queen's Own") with the new large eyes are easily threaded, (even by blind persons,) and work with great ease having improved points, temper and finish: they are made of every length or substance, and for every purpose; the labels are correct likenesses of Her Majesty and his R. Highness Prince Albert in relief on coloured grounds. They can be sent free by post, by any respectable dealer, on receipt of 13 penny stamps for every shilling value.'

So successful did this venture prove that the needle manufacturers began to look for new and more varied pictures to put on their boxes, and, in particular, for coloured prints which would be likely to have a greater appeal at the time on account of their novelty. George Baxter, whose oil-prints were attracting attention, had not been slow in gauging the tastes of the public in this respect: he and his licensees were already producing sheets of coloured prints, about the size of a large postage stamp, which could be used for pasting in scrap-books and many other purposes. These were so much in demand among needle-makers that they were soon referred to as needle-prints, the term by which they are still known today. The little gilt-edged cardboard boxes on to which they were gummed, barely three-eighths of an inch in depth, are most meticulously made. In their day they must have existed in their thousands, but so few have survived the passage of a century that they are always an interesting find for the collector (Plate 16).

During the latter half of the 19th century needle-books came into much more general use, the stiff covers of an earlier day being replaced by embroidery of many kinds, sometimes by punctured-card work, a crude imitation of the delicate canvas work of earlier years (Plate 15). Needle-boxes printed with views of notable buildings or local beauty spots were still sold as souvenirs at spas and holiday resorts, but with the close of the Victorian era a more prosaic age was dawning. The day of the ornamental needle-case was virtually over.

Thread and Thread-winders

IN THE DAYS when prehistoric man lived by hunting, any clothes that he wore were made from the skins of wild beasts, whose sinews provided the thread for sewing. With the introduction of a more settled state of life, the domestication of animals, and the beginnings of agriculture, opportunity was provided for experiments with new materials, in particular for the plaiting and twisting of reeds and rushes, which led to the discovery of weaving. Shepherds, meanwhile, handling the fleece of their sheep, became aware of the exceptional properties of wool which made it possible to draw it out and twist it into thread of almost unlimited length, while the farming members of the community found, in the fibres of flax and other vegetable products, materials equally suitable for the manufacture of cloth. The superiority of woven fabric for many purposes in the home was soon established, and the sedentary occupation of spinning allotted to the female members of the family.

In medieval times, in this country, the spinning and winding of thread was among the most important of domestic occupations. All clothing, bed-linen, curtains and napery had, of necessity, to be made in the home, and the household that could count a highly-skilled spinster among its members was fortunate indeed, for to her could be allotted the difficult task of producing a fine, smooth sewing thread on which the seamstresses might rely for neat and even stitching. Spinning and needlework were much more closely allied then than they are at the present day.

Originally, thread was spun by means of the distaff and spindle (Plate 18), or, as it was termed in Scotland, the rock and reel. The distaff was held under the left arm with a quantity of prepared fleece tied to the top. A short length of wool was first drawn out, twisted by hand and attached to the spindle, which was allowed to hang downwards. The spinster then began to draw out more fibre, regulating the thickness with the fingers of both hands. From time to time, she reached down and, taking hold of the thread, gave it a sharp turn which caused the spindle to revolve and a twist to run up the thread until it was checked by the fingers of the left hand when, to stop the thread unwinding again, the spindle was brought to rest against the skirt. When the spindle neared the ground it was lifted up and the thread wound on to it; after which the spinning continued as before. This primitive method is still in use in remote districts in many parts of the world. Of the five Spanish peasants shown in Plate 18, it will be noted that four are employed with distaff and spindle, while the fifth knits or mends a sock.

To keep a family provided with all the yarn required entailed much work, and in the winter months full advantage had to be taken of every hour of daylight. In some old houses in this country, holes may still occasionally be found bored into the woodwork of a door or newel-post, near to a window where there is a strong light (Plates 19 and 20); these are the holes into which the spinsters of the household inserted their distaffs while spinning, thus leaving their hands free to manipulate the thread.

Most young girls learned to spin as a matter of course, whatever their station in life, and any woman who could produce a yarn of really fine quality was justly proud of her skill and quite prepared to turn it to profit. H. G. Graham, in his *Social Life in Scotland in the 18th Century*, states that, even when calling at large country mansions, the packmen, who carried their goods from door to door, were only too glad to barter their wares for a fine and even thread spun by the lady of the house or her maids. Writing of one such house in the year 1725, he records that, although the Balgarran estate had been in the family for 300 years, it was thought quite natural that the Lady Balgarran should advertise that 'she and her daughters having attained to great perfection in making and twisting sewing thread which is even and white' should offer it for sale at 'from five pence to six shillings an ounce', wrapped in papers bearing the Balgarran coat of arms.

In this country, it was in about 1730 that the flutter of the distaff and spindle gave way to the whirr of the spinning wheel, a change that greatly increased the speed of spinning. An account of the various types of wheel employed, and of the gradual evolution of spinning—a vast subject in itself—is beyond the scope of this book, but some idea of the main processes involved in the production of home-spun thread may be derived from the picture by Velazquez, *Las Hilanderas* (The Spinsters) reproduced in Plate 21.

This picture is of unusual interest, for in spite of the seemingly casual grouping, it is a very careful composition, illustrating the different stages of an age-old craft. Hanging beside the entrance door on the right is a fleece, awaiting the attention of the woman seated in the centre who, with the cards or combs in her hands, is preparing the wool for the distaff. On the extreme left, another woman is drawing aside a heavy curtain to provide more light for the spinster, who draws down some of the fleece from her distaff with one hand as she turns the wheel with the other. The shelf beneath the wheel bends under the weight of a large stone, placed there to keep it steady; resting against this shelf is a cross-reel on to which the spun thread is next wound into a skein. It is in skein form that the thread is taken to be dyed, and the girl entering the room from the right and placing a basket on the ground is, presumably, bringing in a number of newly dyed skeins, to be wound into balls by the woman seated at the revolving winding frame.

A more detailed picture of a cross-reel may be seen in Plate 22. This is an important device, of ancient origin, for winding thread into a skein without an extended movement of the arms. It is held in one hand by the central bar while the thread is taken, in succession, over the four ends of the two short heads or cross-pieces, the circumference of the skein being four times the distance between the two heads. The cross-reel therefore also served as a measuring device; colloquially, it was known as a niddy-noddy, from the rhythmical, up and down movements involved during winding.

The introduction of a treadle for turning the wheel was an improvement on the method shown in Velazquez's picture, as it enabled the two hands to be applied exclusively to the control of the thread. Queen Charlotte, consort of George III, when on a visit to the Duchess of Portland at Bulstrode, in the year 1770, was so taken with the new treadle wheel she saw there that she expressed a wish to have lessons in spinning and desired that a similar type of wheel should be obtained for her. In this same year the Duchess of Northumberland, when staying in Paris, recorded in her diary that she had accompanied Lady Berkeley to the Boulevards 'where I believe she had 100 Spinning Wheels brought into Coach to chuse of'.

For those of ample means spinning was beginning to be regarded as a pleasing drawing-room occupation. As the fashion became established many ingeniously contrived wheels of a decorative nature were made that could be used for spinning flax. The aristocratic young lady in Plate 23, is quite apparently more interested in her elegant table wheel than in the advances of her extravagantly dressed suitor. Of the two demure Englishwomen in Plate 24, it will be noticed that while one is occupied with needlework her companion spins sewing thread on a small wheel placed on her knees. Wordsworth, describing the life of a shepherd's wife living in the remote Grasmere Vale in the early 19th century, wrote:

Thread and Thread-winders

. . . two wheels she had
Of antique form, this large for spinning wool,
That small for flax; and if one wheel had rest
It was because the other was at work.

With the spinning accomplished, and the thread wound on to the skeiner, the housewife had yet another task—to wind her thread off into a suitable form for use. For such work as knitting or tambouring, where a continuous length of yarn was required, the skein might simply be transferred to a large, box-shaped skein-holder standing three or four feet from the floor, which would revolve slowly as the thread was pulled out (Plate 158). If the yarn was to be wound into a ball, a wooden table winder might be used, consisting of four adjustable arms with an upright peg at the end of each and turning on a central pillar (Plate 25). Alternatively, a vertical winder (Plate 26) or a pair of skein winding clamps could be employed (see Chapter 6).

Most needlewomen also possessed a number of small, flat, many-pointed winders of various shapes and sizes which were needed for winding off lengths of thread for sewing and embroidery, in particular for silk which was bought in skeins from the shops (Plate 27). Parson Woodforde, the diarist, who often gave his niece Nancy small presents of sewing accessories, made the following entry in his accounts for October, 1781: 'an ivory thing to wind silk or thread 6d'.

Silk thread, a Chinese invention dating back to a very remote antiquity, differs entirely in its preparation from wool or flax. The cocoon of the silk-worm, from which it is obtained, is formed of a continuous length of fine silk extending, on an average, to several hundred yards. The silk is unwound by immersing the cocoon in hot water, which melts the natural gum binding it together. Several cocoons are wound off at the same time and the silk from them passed through a small eye, the gum causing the fibres to combine in a single strand of silk. This strand forms the raw silk of commerce. Silk thread is made by twisting several strands together, the number and method of twisting varying according to the type of thread required.

Sericulture, though successfully practised in this country, has never become established in England on a large scale, owing chiefly to the unreliability of the climate. The secret of twisting the thread having, however, been learned from Italy in the early 17th century, a mill was built at Derby and was in production before 1750, the raw silk being imported from the countries of southern Europe and from China. Rearing silkworms was a popular domestic pastime in the Victorian era; but the preparation of silk thread is a

31

highly specialised occupation and is outside the sphere of the ordinary needlewoman.

Small flat thread-winders are difficult to date because they were in use unchanged over a long period and, as far as silk is concerned, remained in use until the end of the last century. Many are less than an inch in diameter, neatly cut from mother-of-pearl or ivory, sometimes in sets of six or more fitting into delicately carved boxes. Others are of wood, bone, glass, porcelain or straw-work. In late Georgian and early Victorian work-boxes a multiple winder for holding several different threads is often provided. It consists of a spindle of ivory or bone divided at intervals by four or five discs, and fits into a horizontal compartment (Plate 96). Another multiple winder, much more elaborately made and dating from the late 18th century, may be seen in Plate 28; it stands vertically on a carved foot and is surmounted by a small round box with a conical lid. The foot unscrews so that the hollow spindle can be used as a needle-case while the box at the top holds a cake of wax. On the right of the same illustration is a wooden winder made to take four different threads and hollowed through the centre for the storage of needles. Although this is so simple an appliance, the cylindrical case into which it fits is finely constructed of inlaid ivory and tortoiseshell, an indication of the value that was once placed on devices of this kind.

While in rural districts home-spinning was to continue for many years to come, the gradual increase in the importation of cotton into this country, combined with the inventions of Hargreaves and Arkwright in the latter half of the 18th century, greatly improved the quality and quantity of sewing thread available in the shops. By the beginning of the 19th century, however, it was still being sold by weight and in skein form. An entry in Parson Woodforde's diary in September, 1802, reads: 'A pound of different kinds of Thread for the use of the Family paid o.7.od.' Elizabeth Grant, in her memoirs, also mentions the skeins of sewing thread that were wound off on to improvised cardboard winders; she is writing in the middle of the last century, of the year 1804, at which time she was seven years old:

'One of my employments at this time was to hold the skeins of cotton thread which my Mother wound off neatly on two square pieces of card placed one over the other, so as to form eight corners between which the thread was secured. This cotton thread was a great invention, a wonderful improvement on the flax thread in previous use, which it was difficult to get of sufficient fineness for work, and hardly possible to find evenly spun. When one thinks of the machine spinning of these days, the cotton and flax threads like the fibres of spider's webs, which we produce in tons weight now, we

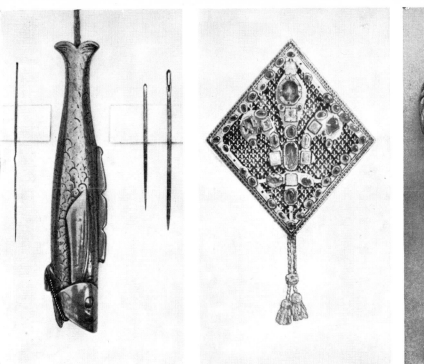

1. 16th-century bronze needle-case in the form of a fish. (*left*) Medieval bronze needle with kink at right-angles to the eye. (*right*) Two early steel needles.　2. So-called *Fermail de St Louis* of silver nielloed, and parcel-gilt set with jewels; probably once an open-ended needle-case.　3. Tubular needle-case from Lapland.

4. Mid 19th-century woodcut of a needle-maker's workshop.

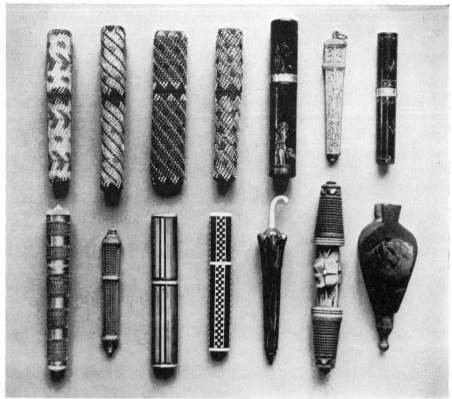

5. (*top row*) Needle-cases of beadwork, *vernis Martin*, silver-gilt and tortoiseshell; (*bottom row*) gold wire on ivory, silver, straw-work, ebony and ivory and wood; 18th and 19th centuries.

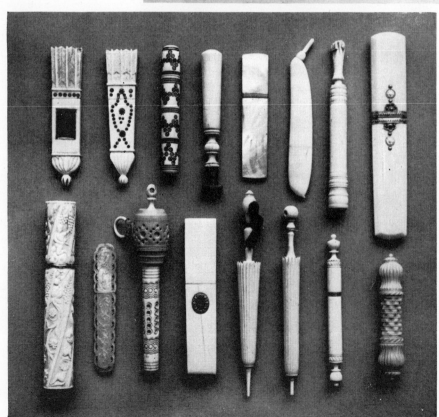

6. Needle-cases of ivory, bone and mother-of-pearl; 18th and 19th centuries.

7. Standing ivory needle-cases in the form of fisherfolk; c. 1700. (*centre*) Ivory thimble and case.

8. (*left*) Silver figure needle-case. (*right*) Standing silver needle-case with thimble top and seal base, and compartments for thread and wafers. (*centre*) 17th-century casket of gold brocade for needles, thimble etc. (*front*) Italian needle-boxes of wood and ivory.

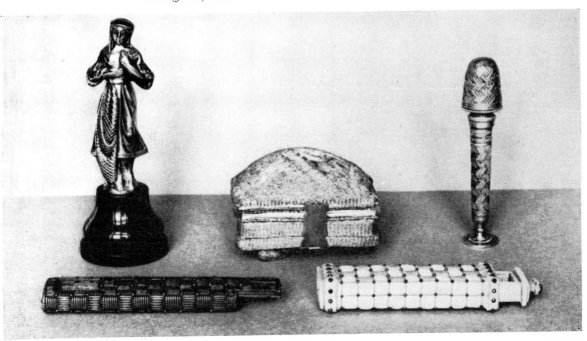

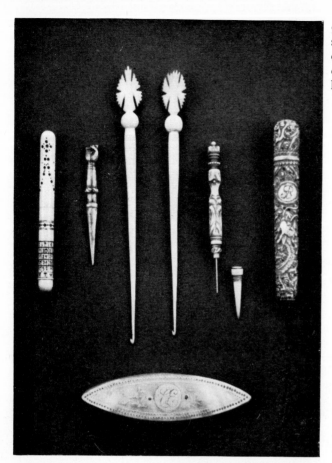

9. Needle-case with perpetual calendar; stiletto; two early crochet hooks; stiletto enclosing pricker and carved Chinese needle-case, all of ivory. (*below*) Mother-of-pearl knotting shuttle.

10. Three bodkin-cases: (*left*) Chinese with silver filigree and enamel; (*centre*) tortoise-shell with piqué; (*right*) silver gilt with silver filigree overlay. Two tortoiseshell and two silver bodkins. (*below*) Two very large bodkins, probably used in dressing the hair, and an unpicking tool, all of tortoise-shell.

11. Mother-of-pearl tambour hook with gold mounts. Bodkin-case of Battersea enamel; *c.* 1755.

12. Print Work, which arose with the production of very fine needles. The picture is 3½ inches in diameter. The stitching is in black and grey threads on white silk; *c.* 1790.

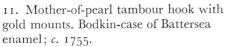

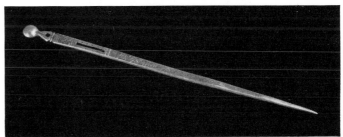

13. Silver bodkin with ear-spoon engraved 'A.W. 1692'. Actual length 6 inches.

14. Two wooden figure needle-cases, and three boxes of inlaid tortoiseshell and mother-of-pearl for holding needles in their packets; early 19th century.

15. (*top row*) Victorian silk pincushion with beads sewn on to perforated card; 18th-century pincushion and emery cushion in bead knitting. (*middle row*) Three needle-books, two with ivory covers and one (*centre*) of punched card with hand written verse. (*bottom row*) Victorian needle-books of perforated card work, and mother-of-pearl; (*centre*) straw-work thread winder.

16. (*top left and right*) Small cardboard needle-boxes, 1″ × 2″, decorated with coloured prints by Baxter and his licensees, and six unused needle-prints.

17. Sampler worked at Bocking, Essex, in 1794. The nine square holes cut in isabelline gauze are darned with coloured silks —an exercise in 'invisible mending' made possible by the introduction of very fine needles. (*See also* Plate 168.)

18. Spanish peasant women spinning in the Mountains of León.

19. Staircase at Moelfre Hall, Llansilin, Denbighshire, showing door frame on the right with holes in which the spinsters placed their distaffs. 20. Staircase at Pont-y-meibon, Llansilin, Denbighshire, with distaff hole in the newel post.

21. *Las Hilanderas*
(The Spinsters), by
Velazquez (1599–
1660)

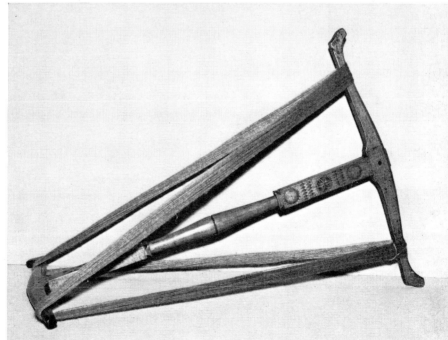

22. Cross-reel or
niddy-noddy showing
method of winding
skein or 'slipping' of
yarn. Length 16⅜".

23. Girl spinning sewing thread. After Pietro Longhi (1702-1785).

24. Woman sewing while her companion spins sewing thread; English, c. 1760.

25. Beechwood skein-winder with extendable arms, clamped to a chair.

26. Vertical wool-winder with cages adjustable to the length of the skein.

27. Thread-winders of ivory, wood and mother-of-pearl.

28. Ball of cotton with cotton-box. Multiple winder with compartment for needles and wax. Silk-winder with interior compartment for needles, and its ivory and tortoise-shell case.

29. Cotton barrels of wood, ivory and bone; late 18th and early 19th centuries.

30. Six ivory cotton barrels, four with handles and two with disc tops for winding up the thread.

31. Carved ivory reels and (*centre*) three reel-holders with mother-of-pearl tops; early 19th century.

32. Victorian revolving reel stand of brass with pincushion and base of blue velvet. 33. Victorian reel stand in the form of a roundabout.

34. (*top row*) Left and right, silver finger protectors; (*centre*) thimbles of wood and horn. (*bottom row*) Brass thimble with thread cutter; four iron thimbles, the second and third are lined with brass, the third and fourth are open topped.

35. Silver plated cup, 5″ in height, made for members of the Tailors' Guild of Nuremberg and dated 1586, an indication of the type of thimble in use at this time.

36. (*top row*) Five silver thimbles: (1 and 2) with hardstone tops, (3) with ornamental punching, (4) with souvenir view of suspension bridge, (5) with rectangular indentations. (*bottom row*) Five silver thimbles: (1) with unusual indentations, (2) with stone-set rim, (3) Chinese hand punched, (4 and 5) for children; (*extreme right*) finely made gold thimble.

37. (*top row*) Three china thimbles; one of mother-of-pearl; the last, of silver engine-turned and enamelled, with moonstone top. (*bottom row*) Six ivory thimbles, (2 and 4) not indented.

38. (*top row*) Thimble cases: (1 and 5) rosewood, (2) brassbound velvet, (3) wood, (4) stained ivory. (*bottom row*) (1 and 5) tortoiseshell veneer, (2) imitation ivory, (3) basket work, (4) stained ivory, with thimble.

39. Seven silver yard measures and (*top centre*) late 18th-century silver filigree thimble forming a cover for a blue cut-glass scent bottle.

40. Seven turned and carved ivory yard measures, and two made from natural shells.

41. Three examples of yard measure and pincushion combined; lathe-turned and decorated bone.

42. Yard measures: (*top row*) three in imitation ivory, and one of ivory and ebony with silver piqué; (*bottom row*) (1) imitation ivory, (2) painted wood, (3) Tunbridge ware, (4) shell veneer; (*centre*) ivory and ebony case with yard measure base and compartments for needles, thimble and thread.

may indeed wonder at the difficulties in needlework overcome by our mothers.'

Manufacturers, meanwhile, continued in their efforts to devise new methods of winding their thread in a more convenient form before sale to the public. Cotton, in particular, was the cause of much trouble as it was less tractable than silk or wool and on an ordinary flat winder was apt to become loose and entangled if the end was not securely fastened. It was this fact, no doubt, that brought about the invention of the cotton barrel in the latter part of the 18th century. A cotton barrel is composed of three parts; the hollow container itself, a spindle attached to a small reel on which the thread is wound, and a flat screw-on lid with a central hole through which the top of the spindle protrudes (Plate 29). The cotton is drawn out through a small hole in the side of the barrel and can be wound back by a turn of the spindle. It was an extremely practical device, as the thread, being enclosed, was kept clean and could not become unwound or entangled with other objects in a work-box. When the barrel was empty the lid was unscrewed and the spindle sent back to the makers for refilling.

As may be seen, cotton barrels may be broad or slender, plain or decorated: some are made of wood, but the majority are turned from ivory or bone, occasionally painted, or ornamented with mosaic inlay. Those found in work-boxes vary in height from three-quarters of an inch to just over two inches, but for ordinary household sewing in a large establishment wooden barrels four or more inches in height were made (Plate 44). In Plate 30 there are four barrels of an unusual design, each one being provided with a handle attached to the spindle by which the cotton was wound up. In front are two barrels of yet another type; here the flat disc-like top turns the spindle, and the base unscrews for refilling.

Reels similar in shape to those used today, but made from bone or ivory, are also to be found in late 18th-century work-boxes. They were turned by hand, and are generally carved or otherwise ornamented on the top. Before filling the reels, the maker fixed to the body of each a label with his name and the number of the thread, so that when empty it could be returned for re-winding. Being far less complicated in construction than the cotton barrels, bone reels were cheaper to produce; the main drawback here was that there was no way of fixing the loose end of the thread which was continually becoming unwound. In the two exceptionally elaborate reels in Plate 31 this difficulty has been overcome by the provision of a carved rose that screws in and out of the top, securing the end of the cotton firmly in place.

Within a few years of the opening of the 19th century mechanical methods of winding had developed sufficiently to allow sewing cotton to be sold ready wound in the same manner as string is sold today. Elizabeth Grant records that by 1806 'the prettily wound cotton balls had already superseded the skeins', thus freeing her from the constant necessity of sitting with hands outstretched at the request of her numerous aunts and other elderly relatives. For holding single balls, small boxes with a hole in the lid, resembling miniature string boxes, were made (Plate 28), and in the elaborate fitted work-boxes of the period the bone or ivory barrels and reels were replaced by cotton balls in numbered sizes. In the saffian work-box in Plate 97 with dated fittings commemorating the coronation of William and Adelaide in 1831, a row of these balls appears. Flat winders were needed only for silk at this period.

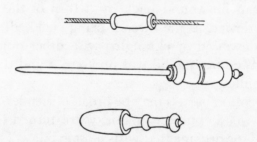

Fig. 4. *(centre)* The Reeling Pin, 'which some call a Knave or Reeling prick which is for the Spool to run or turn upon whilst it is reeling upon the Reel'. The pin with the spool of thread on it was held in one hand, the cross-reel *(see* Plate 22) in the other. *(above)* The Bead 'to draw the Yarn through that it cut not the winder's fingers' when winding a clew or ball. *(below)* The Nogg 'to begin to wind the Clew on', so that, when completed, the yarn can be drawn from the centre.

By the early years of Queen Victoria's reign the continuing development of machinery enabled manufacturers for the first time to sell their cotton wound on to wooden reels made speedily and in quantity. The problem of securing the thread was solved by the simple expedient of cutting a notch in the wood, while, even more important, the need for refilling was dispensed with, as, when empty, the reels could be thrown away, an innovation to which, incidentally, our more thrifty ancestors accustomed themselves only gradually. In some of these early reels the central hole is bored only part of the way through, the maker's name and the number of the cotton, surrounding a portrait of the young Queen, being embossed in the wood in bold relief on the top. Wooden reels were not, however, considered sufficiently decorative for a fitted sewing-box or work-table; for these, sets of ornamental reel-holders were made, composed of an ivory or bone base and a flat top, usually of shell and often carved in a flower petal design. Base and top are joined by a metal tube and pin which can be pulled apart, or by an ivory rod into which the top is screwed, thus allowing the reel to be slipped on and off as required (Plate 31).

In spite of the development of the factory system, a great deal of clothing continued to be made in the home, and for the care of household linen a good seamstress needed five or six reels of white cotton in varying grades for the different processes involved. For such everyday use, another type of cotton-box was now made; it contained a circle of pegs over which the new wooden reels could be placed as required, the thread from each reel being pulled out from a separate hole with the number of the cotton beside it. Elaborate revolving reel stands, holding cottons of many grades and colours, and preserved under their own glass domes, belong to this period, but went out of fashion at the end of the Victorian era (Plate 32).

There is also a humbler type of revolving stand which, perhaps because of its fascination for successive generations of children, has survived until comparatively recent times. Substantially made of metal or wood, it took the form of a roundabout or merry-go-round, the centre of attraction of countless village flower shows and country fairs (Plate 33). With its reels of bright coloured cottons held in place by vertical metal rods and surmounted by a pincushion, it was still to be seen in the first half of this century standing on many a cottage mantelpiece in this country.

3

Thimbles, Yard Measures, and Miscellaneous Sewing Accessories

THE WORD THIMBLE is derived from the Old English *thymel*, meaning a thumb stall. It was originally a small bell-shaped cap of leather, made to be worn on the thumb in sewing. Although this type of primitive protection continued in use in remote and isolated districts until quite recent times, the metal thimble displaced it in more civilised countries at a very early period. Thimbles of bronze have been found on the sites of Greek and Roman cities, such as Pompeii and Herculaneum, which were destroyed in A.D. 79. They can be divided into two types: one heavy, cast, and with the indentations irregularly placed; the other finely made from sheet metal, with indentations more neatly arranged and occasionally having an open top. These open-topped thimbles still continue in use, particularly among tailors, as they have the advantage of leaving the sensitive tip of the finger exposed to assist in picking up pins, needles or thread.

A cast bronze ring, about a quarter of an inch deep, with three rows of indentations arranged diamond-wise, served a similar purpose and could be worn as comfortably as any ordinary finger ring (Fig. 5). This modified thimble was probably cast in a stone mould and, the casting having been trimmed up, the indentations added by hand. It must not be supposed, however, that Greek and Roman craftsmen were limited to such primitive methods; they were well acquainted with die stamping, turning and spinning metal objects in a lathe, and also with casting by the waste-wax process, by which thimbles requiring very little further treatment could be produced.

Although the thimble is so necessary an item in sewing equipment, archaeological sources in this country have provided little material from the middle ages which can be dated with reasonable accuracy. It is nevertheless clear, from an example recovered during the systematic excavation of Weoley Castle, near Birmingham, that in the 15th century the indentations were

36

already being made on a lathe (Fig. 5). The thimble, fixed in a chuck which fitted exactly its internal diameter, was revolved while a knurled wheel was pressed against it into a series of shallow grooves guiding the revolving wheel.

A silver thimble is mentioned in the will of Dame Philippa Brudenell, in 1532; it was bequeathed to the wife of her stepson.[1] Evidence of advances in manufacturing methods during this century may be gauged from a cup, fashioned in the form of a thimble, five inches high and probably one of a set, that was made to the order of members of the Tailors' Guild of Nuremberg in 1586 (Plate 35). It is of brass close plated with silver and, apart from its somewhat elaborate ornamentation, is presumably a replica of an ordinary thimble of the time. The indentations are here again knurled in, but not in

Fig. 5. (*top*) Bronze thimble ring, and thimble from the ruins of Pompeii. (*centre*) Two heavy bronze thimbles of the Roman period, and a 15th-century thimble from the site of Weoley Castle, Birmingham. (*below*) A 17th-century silver bodkin.

single rows; several knurled wheels were mounted together on the same tool, a method which has been developed in modern days to great perfection. It should also be noted that the inscription and much of the decoration has been rolled on in the same manner. Another point of interest is that the base of the cup was made separately and soldered on to the body, which is of sheet metal bent to a tube, with a soldered seam. Thimbles of uncertain date made in this way may be seen in the British Museum; they were probably soldered with tin which has perished, causing the joints to open and thus revealing the method of manufacture.

In an inventory of the possessions of Queen Elizabeth I there is mention of 'a nedell case of cristall garnysshed with silver gilt, with twoo thimbles in it'. Although no mention of the material is made, the thimbles would no doubt have been in keeping with their costly container. Among the personal possessions of the Queen preserved at Burghley House, Stamford, is a gold thimble, with indentations but without ornament.

In 1663, James Dillon, the future Lord Roscommon, after one of his frequent visits to the Verneys at Claydon, sent two thimbles to Mary Verney and her cousin Doll Leeke 'that the one should not hurt a fine finger by the

---

[1] *The Brudenells of Deene*, by Joan Wake, Cassell, 1953.

making of handkerchiefs, nor the other receive a prick in working my lady's buttons'. Whether these were of silver is not stated but, with the large amount of domestic sewing that was necessary in former centuries, thimbles wore out quickly, and as the Verney household, in common with humbler establishments, was dependent on the infrequent visits of pedlars for all objects of this kind, to the two young girls a thimble of any metal may well have been an acceptable present.

A silver thimble of the reign of Charles II may be seen in the British Museum; but, in general, examples of gold or silver dating from this period are extremely rare. This may be due, in part, to the custom of all sections of the community, during the Civil War, of making gifts of articles of gold and silver to the Royalist or Parliamentary forces, a practice which earned the latter the title of 'Thimble and Bodkin Army'. Though the term was ironical, there is no doubt that many gold and silver thimbles were in fact melted down at this period, as they have been in more recent times in aid of patriotic and other causes.

In 1696 a Dutch mechanic, John Lofting, introduced the recently invented art of sand casting into England. Having found a suitable sand in the district, he set up a workshop in Islington where he produced large quantities of cast thimbles. It must not be overlooked that these thimbles, as taken from the mould, were far from finished: they were only the rough blanks on which much work was still required. It is doubtful, therefore, if the method Lofting employed was superior to that already in use in other parts of this country. Daniel Defoe in an account of his journeys through Great Britain, in the opening years of the 18th century, makes mention of two water-mills that he came upon at Great Marlow, 'one for making of thimbles, a work excellently well finished and which performed to admiration'.

At this period thimbles for all ordinary household sewing were made of brass or steel, or sometimes of a combination of the two. An open-topped steel thimble might be lined with brass (Plate 34), or a thin brass thimble with a smooth top might be surrounded with a broad indented steel band to take the pressure of the needle. Even brass thimbles could be delicately patterned, while those of steel, with a double row of brightly cut facets immediately above the rim, could be a most suitable gift for a lady. In October, 1763, Parson Woodforde recorded in his diary that he gave to his sister Jenny a present of needles, pins and two steel thimbles which he bought for her in Oxford. Alternatively, a silver thimble with a steel top might be obtained; the top, stamped with indentations, was soldered on, the work being so neatly executed that the addition of the base metal is barely discernible. Among the long list of objects stocked by a Holborn toy-seller 'at the Green Parrot near Chancery Lane' in 1762 were 'steel topt and other thimbles'.

It is with those thimbles which were never intended to withstand the wear and tear of daylong sewing, but were reserved for fine needlework and social occasions, that the collector will be mainly concerned. These may be the work of skilled craftsmen and their interest lies not in their age, for they are often extremely difficult to date, but in their seemingly endless variety. Many silver thimbles are engraved with a commemorative inscription or a posy running just above the rim; it may have been engraved, but was more usually rolled on, the pattern being cut intaglio on the edge of a narrow steel roller and pressed into the thimble as it revolved on a chuck in the lathe.

As an alternative to the steel top, many silver thimbles were capped with hardstones, such as amethyst, avanturine, cornelian or moonstone (Plate 36). These indented caps were made and supplied by lapidaries and mounted in bezels on the top of the thimble; the fine indentations on the metal sides were intended for light sewing, the stone tops for more stubborn material. Colour occurs so rarely in silver thimbles that special mention should, perhaps, be made of the example in the bottom row of Plate 36 that has a stout rim in which opaque stones of differing shades have been set flush with the metal.

One of the most charming of all needlework toys is a tall silver thimble dating from the late 18th century, the lower part of open filigree, with a small oval cartouche neatly engraved with a monogram; it screws on to a round silver base on which is mounted a miniature scent bottle of blue Bristol glass (centre Plate 39). With some thimbles of this type a crest or monogram is engraved under the base to serve as a seal; it was not an uncommon practice, however, for ladies of the period to press the top of their thimbles into the wax with which they sealed their letters.

For children, nests of thimbles were made fitting one on top of another and increasing gradually in size, to allow for growth. The smallest of these might be less than three-eighths of an inch in diameter at the rim, for as a child was expected to be able to embroider an elaborate sampler at seven or eight years old instruction in stitchery began at a very early age. There are a few known examples, dating from the 19th century, of samplers worked with plain letters and numerals by children of four years old. The small silver thimble in Plate 36 was certainly intended for a child of about this age; it is impressed with the motto 'Forget-me-not'.

In the early Victorian era, there arose a fashion for ornamenting the sides of thimbles with representations in relief of famous buildings, bridges and other well-known landmarks; they were sold as souvenirs to tourists who were increasing in number owing to the developments in railway travelling. The portion of the thimble so decorated was stamped separately from a die in a piece of flat silver, and rolled round and seamed before being soldered to the upper functional part.

With regard to the hallmarking of gold and silver thimbles, all those made before 1738 should have been hallmarked; in fact they were not, as the regulation imposed by the Assay Offices was never strictly enforced. After 1738, both gold and silver thimbles were exempted; but in 1792 the exemption was withdrawn from silver thimbles if over fine pennyweights. Nevertheless, in order to guarantee the standard of thimbles of less weight, manufacturers could, if they so desired, always have the hallmark applied, and in many cases did so, an option which has remained available to the present day.

There are a very large number of thimbles of great interest although made from materials of much less intrinsic value; many are of bone or ivory, the latter sometimes with most delicate lathe decoration, and smooth and pleasant in use. Their shape will provide little indication of their date: those made during the last three or four centuries may be either short and flat topped, or long, tapering and domed, according to the fashion of the time or the whim of the maker. Mother-of-pearl thimbles came from France; glass from Bohemia or Venice. Wooden thimbles came from Germany and Austria, where they were bought as souvenirs by tourists (Plate 34), but they are by no means common as wood is a soft material unsuitable for practical use in sewing. Complete thimbles without indentations, fashioned from horn, ivory or tortoiseshell, may occasionally be found; they are, in fact, finger guards and were worn on the first finger of the left hand to protect it from the continual prick of the needle's point. When these guards were made of metal, part of the top was cut away diagonally, leaving only the rim entire.

In tambour work, a thimble of a somewhat similar shape was used, made from a piece of metal rolled round without being joined, so that it would expand to the required size. It was worn on the forefinger of the right hand; the top, cut on the slope, and with a notch at the highest point, guided the needle and served to press down the material as the stitch was drawn to the upper surface.

Very decorative thimbles, of enamel on copper, were made at Battersea, and at Bilston in Staffordshire; the side was reserved for decoration in bright colours and a piece of stout brass let into the top to take the pressure of the needle. A charming enamelled silver thimble of comparatively recent date, seen in Plate 37, is remarkable for the effective use of rose engine-turning the scene is a reindeer drawing a sledge, in silhouette, through a snow landscape; the sky is in transparent enamel and, over the engine turning, gives a pleasing suggestion of the aurora borealis. The serviceable part of the thimble is an indented moonstone neatly set in the top.

China thimbles were not made in any quantity until the second quarter of the 19th century when, for a time, they became extremely popular. Of the few that bear the maker's mark those of the Royal Worcester factory are the most common. As with those enamelled on copper, the top only may be indented, to allow for the decoration of the sides, usually with flowers or birds. Many, given as presents, soon found their way into drawing room corner-cupboards and cabinets, as they were too frail for general use, although the smoothness of a china thimble was said to be of great advantage when sewing silk as there were few irregularities to catch up the fine threads.

This long-established practice of giving thimbles as presents had led to the introduction of small ornamental cases to contain them (Plate 38). Gold thimbles were often provided with shagreen covered boxes, while those of silver had their own caskets with filigree decoration. Chelsea enamelled thimbles were enclosed in matching enamelled cases. Eggs turned from ivory with naturalistic painting or covered with fine beadwork also belong to the 18th century. Small cylindrical boxes of rare woods or Tunbridge ware occasionally occur. Some took the form of an acorn or carrot; the acorn may stand on a turned base, the carrot may contain an emery cushion in the screw-on lid. Octagonal boxes, veneered with tortoiseshell and mother-of-pearl, were similar in appearance to the needle-cases with sloping lids which came in with the 1800s; some, indeed, were large enough to provide room for graduated packets of needles as well as a thimble. A miniature brass-bound trunk covered with velvet is characteristic of the Victorian era.

Old thimbles found in antique shops are almost invariably of a small size, from which it is often assumed that fingers were formerly more pointed and delicate than they are at the present day. This may be true in part, but it must be remembered that a great many thimbles were needed in the past for children and young girls, and it is these thimbles that in modern times tend to remain unsold.

In earlier centuries every household possessed its own carefully marked wooden measuring stick, or meteyard as it was then termed, handed down in many cases through successive generations. Apart from its general domestic uses it was of particular value to the mistress of the house in ensuring that the travelling salesman, who called at the door with ribbons, laces and fabrics of all kinds, was giving correct measure for her money. From it, also, the housewife made her own yard-measures which she used for needlework, marking off the feet and inches on a length of tape or ribbon. When the ribbon became worn and frayed a new length was marked off, not from the old ribbon, but from the wooden stick, thus ensuring that accurate measurements were maintained. It is from these practices that the modern use of the word yardstick is derived, denoting a gauge by which values may be assessed.

Ribbon measures winding into small receptacles were in use in the early part of the 17th century and were thought of sufficient importance to be named among minor bequests. On the death of Lady Isham at Claydon in 1667 we are told: 'Her ample pockets abounded with dainty implements', among them a silver measure which she left to her sister Sherard. On early ribbon measures figures seldom appear: long and short lines represent feet and inches, and may be marked with ink or embroidery. The delicately carved ivory basket illustrated in Plate 40 has a ribbon marked with lines of stitching in green silk. Measures with hand-written figures are found belonging to the 18th century, but they were gradually replaced by stencilled and printed ribbons in late Georgian and Victorian times.

On some measures inches are ignored and letters instead of figures are used to indicate fractions of a yard: thus an old ribbon may be marked N, HQ, Q, H and Y, standing for Nail, Half Quarter, Quarter, Half and Yard. A nail is a measure of two and a quarter inches used principally for measuring cloth. The markings of old foreign measures are more difficult to identify as the metric system did not come into use until 1799 and before that date measurements varied considerably in different localities. The English yard, however, has been a standard measurement ever since King Henry I decided that it should be the length of his arm.

In many countries the ribbons were wound into small shells (Plate 40), but though simple in form these shell measures were by no means easy to construct; to fit a smoothly running spindle into a cowrie required considerable skill, and only the frailest of silk ribbons would roll into so small a container. A measure of exceptionally delicate construction may be seen in Plate 42. Though only five-eighths of an inch in height and half an inch in diameter, it is ten-sided and is composed of alternating light and dark slips of the iridescent ormer or ear-shell.

A yard measure may often be combined with a needle-case, a pincushion (Plate 41), or a thread-waxer the latter always an important accessory in former centuries. For coarse work beeswax was used; the countrywoman obtained it, most probably, from her own hive; but in the towns it was sold in cakes decorated with stars and other motifs cut from gold paper (Plate 43). As the natural wax was liable to stain white thread, a more refined white wax was sold for sewing light coloured fabrics. In the elegant sewing boxes of the late 18th century it will usually be found in small, flat cakes pressed between two circular discs of carved ivory or mother-of-pearl; in fitted Victorian work-tables, it may be moulded into cylindrical form with top and base matching the reel holders. An egg-shaped case turned from a Coquilla nut, with elaborate pierced and lathe decoration, may also be found to contain wax; wooden boxes, carved in the form of fruit, which have been much sought after by collectors in recent years, were used for a similar purpose (Plate 44).

These, with other containers, went out of fashion in the latter part of the last century when smooth machine-made thread became so readily obtainable that, for all ordinary domestic sewing, waxing was rendered unnecessary. For tailors, cobblers and sail-makers, however, it was still essential.

The sailor, with long months or even years at sea, had his own character-istic sewing tools which he carried in his ditty-bag or box. A rolled-up hussif contained needles, thimble and hanks of thread for mending, darning and sewing on buttons. His pincushion, made most likely by his wife or sweetheart, was probably heart-shaped, with 'Good Luck' pricked out in pins and coloured beads—a mascot to bring him back safely from his voyage. For making and mending nets he needed shuttles and gauges of various sizes (see Chapter 9). In the days of sailing ships he required an implement known as a sailor's 'palm', which took the place of a thimble and enabled him to use the full force of his hand when stitching the strong sail cloth with heavily waxed thread; it consisted of an indented metal plate set in a leather band worn across the palm of the hand, with a hole through which the thumb could be slipped, thus keeping it in position. He would also need a sail-smoother, a tool about 4 to 6 inches in length, fashioned from wood, bone or ivory, the handle sometimes ornamented with carving or other decoration. Its spade-shaped blade was used for smoothing and flattening the long seams of the sail canvas.

Of the various egg-shaped objects associated with sewing, two yet remain to be mentioned: darning eggs and hand coolers. The distinguishing character-istic of a darning egg is its lightness; to hold a heavy object in one's hand during long hours of mending would obviously have been inconvenient and tiring. Darning eggs were therefore made from light woods, sometimes of Tunbridge ware, and also of horn. A highly polished immature coconut, owing to its extreme lightness, might also serve a similar purpose (Plate 45). At the beginning of the last century earthenware, so-called china, darning eggs decorated with representations of sailing ships and sentimental scenes were sold as souvenirs at holiday resorts; they were also obtainable at fairs and exhibitions, bearing popular christian names or, to special order, the full name of the recipient and the date (Plate 44). Glove darning sticks are either tapered or may consist of a short rod with a small egg at each end. A box with six compartments containing a set of boxwood eggs of different sizes, and with its original label '*Oeufs à Gants*', is in the Pinto Collection of Wooden Bygones.

Hand coolers, in contrast, were made from natural stones: Derbyshire spar and serpentine rock or marble, which, as bad conductors of heat, in ordinary conditions always remain cool. While, as is often stated, they may have been used by young ladies who wished to appear calm and collected when offering their hand on social occasions, they had a very definite place in a work-box. A careful needlewoman, particularly when occupied with white work, took pains to prevent her fingers becoming hot and moist, and so staining either thread or material, by taking the cold stone egg in her hand from time to time. Powder sprinklers filled with French chalk are, for this same reason, often to be found among sewing accessories and may take various forms (Plate 46). Some, however, preferred the small bottles of scent which are included in many sewing outfits, the spirit being used not only for its fragrance, but to clear the fingers of grease, and to cool the hand by its rapid evaporation.

4

Scissors and Knives

SCISSORS, though so important an item of sewing equipment, are among the less common of surviving needlework implements, for they are too useful to be allowed to remain idle with other accessories in a work-box that has fallen into disuse, and so become worn out or broken in the course of years. There are two main types of scissors: those that work with a spring action, now commonly called shears (Plates 47 and 55), and those with pivoted blades such as are used for most ordinary purposes today. Both types were in use in Roman times and are usually described as having been made of iron, but as steel and its properties were already well known it is reasonable to assume that the blades, at least, were made of the harder metal. In this country pivotal scissors did not come into general use until the late Middle Ages.

Spring scissors were nevertheless retained for purposes to which they were specially suited: by weavers, for snipping the loose ends of threads; by fullers, for trimming the pile of woollen material; and by tailors and seamstresses, for cutting cloth. The shape and proportions of old scissors are always worthy of a close scrutiny, for they usually serve some definite end which may not be discernible without careful examination. It was, for instance, no mere whim of the maker that the snake-like handles of the Chinese scissors in Plate 49 should be large enough to take the full breadth of the hand, while the blades are but two inches in length; they were made for tufting rugs and similar processes where constant clipping was needed, at the same time allowing the free use of the fingers without laying the implement down. Though made of iron, a narrow strip of steel has been welded on to the blades to give a hardened cutting edge. Snipping scissors of this kind were also used by lace-makers.

By the latter part of the 16th century considerable advances had been made by Continental scissorsmiths in the manufacture of more delicate implements suitable for embroidery for which there was a growing demand, due largely to the increasing popularity of fine cut-work—a type of needlework that was to remain in fashion for more than a century. In this country scissor-

45

smiths are mentioned in the register of the Cutlers' Company at the time of its incorporation in Sheffield in 1624, but it was some years before the finest sewing scissors were readily obtainable here. In 1649, Susan Verney, in a letter to her brother Ralph who was in exile in Paris, writes: 'Pray brother lett mee beg a payer of very leetle french sisers of you.' Nevertheless, more than a century later, in 1765, Horace Walpole sent over from Paris a pair of scissors, belonging to some French friends, to have them copied in London, as the craftsmanship of this country was by then considered superior.

Some of the most decorative scissors of the 18th century were enclosed in cases of iron with gilt or enamel decoration (Plate 48). In Italy the smooth surface of the metal might be intricately patterned with niello work on the handles and also on the outer sides of the 'cut'. Spain was celebrated for its finely damascened and etched steel scissors made by the craftsmen of Toledo, whose skill in decorating swords had been handed down from generation to generation. An unusual pair of steel scissors, found, somewhat surprisingly, in an English work-table, may be seen in Plate 50. The shank is made in the form of a crucifix with the limbs and features of the figure etched on the metal; the beardless Christ suggests a Russian origin, and it is probable that they were once used in some religious establishment for embroidery or for teaching children to sew. Even more elaborate are the pierced steel scissors in Plate 53, the design of the handle being particularly pleasing, as it is so perfectly balanced that at first glance it appears to be symmetrical.

Implements from the East may be still more ornate. The long, hollow steel blades of the Persian cloth scissors in Plate 51 are damascened with gold, the handles of bronze carefully shaped to fit finger and thumb, though much too small for the average modern hand. Bird or stork scissors (Plate 52), with gilded plumage and the beak forming the blades, are also Eastern in origin, but have been manufactured in many countries in more recent times. Dolphin scissors, with the fish of ivory and other materials curving gracefully to form the connection between the handle and the cut, were also made.

In contrast, scissors plain in themselves might be contained in decorative cases of shagreen, galuchat, filigree or delicately painted enamel. Like other sewing implements they were sold at the many toy-sellers' shops that were springing up in London at the beginning of the 18th century. In Queen Anne's time a toy-shop was the equivalent of the modern gift shop: the word 'toy' at this period did not necessarily mean a child's plaything; it was used to denote any small article, useful or ornamental, and often of an extravagant and costly nature. Among the objects illustrated in an advertisement of a toy-seller's wares published in 1712 there are scissors and thimbles in decorated cases with chain and clasp to swing from the waist, and there is also an etui, exactly similar in type to the examples illustrated in Plate 88, for which, as may be seen, scissors with ingeniously contrived folding handles were made. 'These and many other usefull Curiosities', it is stated, 'are made and sold Wholesale and Retail at the Great Toy Shop next ye Dogg Tavern in Ludgate Street very reasonable by G. Willdey.'

Another more famous shop where needlework accessories could be purchased was Deard's in Pall Mall. Both Garrick and Horace Walpole refer to 'Deard's deluding Toys'. Lady Mary Wortley Montagu, in her *Town Eclogues*, also mentions Deard's: describing one of the elaborate chatelaines that were then in fashion, she writes:

> *A myrtle foliage round the thimble case;*
> *Jove, Jove himself does on the scissors shine . . .*

From France in the late 18th century came the frail pearl-handled embroidery scissors (Plate 56), sometimes accompanied by thimble and needlecase of the same material. Similar implements were fashioned with handles of ivory and also of silver, the scissors protected by a sheath with chased or filigree decoration. The finely pointed steel blades of the gold-handled embroidery scissors in Plate 54 fit into a sheath of the more valuable metal; almost every pair of sewing scissors had its sheath to prevent the sharp points from damaging the linings of pockets and work-bags, a precaution that was dispensed with only gradually as work-boxes came into more general use. In Jane Austen's *Sense and Sensibility* Edward Ferrars, it will be remembered, when breaking the news of his brother's marriage with Lucy Steele, 'took up a pair of scissors that lay there . . . spoiling both them and their sheath by cutting the latter to pieces as he spoke.' During the first half of the 19th century silver or silver-gilt handles moulded in a floral or foliage pattern were made in considerable quantities, and at the time of the Great Exhibition in 1851 handles surmounted by a crown were an obvious attraction.

The popularity of Carrickmacross lace, introduced about 1820, brought with it a demand for small embroidery scissors of a kind now generally known as lace scissors. They may be distinguished by a small lump of metal that is attached to the point of one of the blades. Carrickmacross work is composed of a layer of fine cambric laid on machine-made net. When the pattern has been outlined with stitching, much of the cambric must be cut away close to the stitches, leaving the design *appliqué* on the net. It is for this delicate operation that the special scissors are needed, the lump of metal on the lower blade ensuring that the net background is not accidentally snipped.

Buttonhole scissors are a comparatively modern invention, but there is a small tool, occasionally to be found in an old work-box, that is sometimes described as a buttonhole cutter, though not always very efficient in this capacity. It is about three inches in length, with a handle of wood or ivory, its steel shaft terminating in a spade-shaped blade which, to be effective, had to be extremely sharp (Plate 50); in America the blade was sometimes set at one side of the handle so that the implement resembled a tomahawk in miniature. It was generally known as a seam knife, as it was used for cutting the stitches when unpicking the seams of old or discarded garments. The rich silks, velvets and brocades, of which many articles of clothing worn by the wealthier classes in the 17th and 18th centuries were composed, were far too costly to be thrown aside when the garments themselves became outmoded or outworn. Coats, petticoats, waistcoats and breeches, therefore, were taken to pieces, and portions of the fabric salvaged for making into pincushions, sweet bags and similar objects.

At the other end of the scale, among the less affluent, poverty and thrift alike demanded that no good material, however plain, should be wasted. Dresses and suits showing signs of wear were carefully unpicked, seam by seam, to be turned and re-sewn, the whole garment reappearing as new. To open a seam a preliminary loosening with a pair of scissors was necessary, the two edges were then held apart in the left hand, on one side with the thumb and forefinger, and on the other side with the remaining three fingers. The seam knife was held in a vertical position in the right hand and brought down in a series of quick, light strokes, severing the thread of the loosened stitches without touching the material on either side.

The spade-shaped cutter disappeared towards the end of the 18th century when folding pocket knives became generally obtainable, the short blade, originally intended for cutting quill pens, proving equally suitable for opening seams. A folding knife is usually included among the fitments of Victorian work-tables and sewing-boxes.

Pins, Pincushions and Pin-boxes

PINS, LIKE NEEDLES, are such necessary objects for use in everyday life that means of making them were found in very early times. Like needles, they were at first fashioned from thorns and fish bones, or carved from slips of wood, bone or ivory, until, eventually, with the increasing use of metals, they were made of bronze. Early metal pins were the work of individual craftsmen and were forged by hand. For pointing, an implement known as a pinner's bone, actually the metatarsal bone of a horse, was employed. At the squared end of the example illustrated in Plate 58 two grooves can be seen, into either of which the end of a pin was placed to steady it while the surplus metal was filed away; the marks made by the file, running diagonally across the grooves, are also visible.

The formation of the heads, at this period, varied according to the whim of the maker. The shanks also differed greatly in size: the largest of the pins shown to the left of the pinner's bone measures no less than six inches. Implements of this length must be regarded not so much as an aid to needlework as a substitute for it; they were intended mainly for fixing folds and draperies and for securing garments of all kinds. As, in these circumstances, the sharp points could be extremely dangerous, small sheaths were provided, having a hole by which they could be attached by thread to the clothing in the required positions, so that the points might be inserted into them. A number of these pins with their sheaths, found on the site of a medieval pin-maker's workshop, are shown in Plate 59; on one sheath, it may be noticed, there is a claw-shaped device for fixing it to the dress.

It was soon found that, for small pins such as those associated with household sewing, it was more practical to make the head separately from the shank. For this purpose a length of wire was coiled, in a lathe, round another wire of the same diameter as the pin. The coil was then cut up into pieces of two turns, and one of these pieces was slipped along the pin until it was held by a slight flattening at the top where it was secured by soldering with tin.

49

There is an early example of a pin of this type on Plate 58, and in the centre of Plate 59 is a short length of fine coiled wire prepared for cutting up into heads. An objection to this kind of head was that the ends of the coil were rough and apt to catch in the material; this defect was remedied later by stamping the head into a smooth round ball.

It is probable that, as with needles, the making of pins became one of the activities fostered by the English monasteries before the Reformation. Chaucer, in 1387, gave more than a hint of this when, in describing the 'wanton and merye' friar in the Prologue to the *Canterbury Tales*, he wrote:

> *His typet was ay stuffed ful of knyves*
> *And pynnes, for to give to faire wyves.*

In these early days, any woman would have appreciated a gift of pins, which were a great expense even to the more well-to-do. To the poor they were still a luxury. This fact is well exemplified in the *Autobiography of Thomas Raymond*, in which he describes how, in the reign of Henry VII, a monk of Westminster, having been invited to a masque at Court, decided the next morning to revisit the scene of splendour; but on reaching the Palace he found that the Court had already removed, so that all he now saw was 'bare walls, dust and rubbish, and the tables and trestles throwne about . . . and in one corner a poore old man with a piece of candle in his hand—lookeing for pynnes.'

Attempts that had been made in Richard III's reign to restrict the importation of foreign pins into England had not proved successful; but in 1543, Henry VIII, in a determined effort to encourage home manufacture, passed an Act 'for the True Making of Pynnes', fixing a maximum price for them in this country. His Queen, Catherine Howard, nevertheless, is said to have favoured French pins, which were renowned for their fineness. The number of pins considered necessary for a lady's requirements at this period is astonishing: no fewer than 10,000 were provided for Henry's young daughter, Mary Tudor. In the reign of Queen Elizabeth I a large and well-filled pincushion was an essential toilet accessory for every woman of rank. The Queen herself received, among her New Year gifts in 1562, an elaborately embroidered pinpillow. In a contemporary painting of one of her maids of honour, the Countess of Southampton, a table is represented on which are set out for display her jewel casket and jewels, and with them a large pincushion completely filled with pins—a clear indication of the value placed on such a possession in those days.

After the Reformation, Gloucestershire became the main centre of the pin-making industry, though numerous other local manufactories are known to have existed. The status of the London pinners was greatly enhanced when, in 1568, they were united with the Worshipful Company of Girdlers, and it is in consequence of the granting of this charter that a portrait of Queen Elizabeth I sometimes appeared on packets of pins made in the London area.

In France, pin-making had long been centred in Paris, where more than a thousand craftsmen were employed in the industry. By the rules of their trade, no master could open there more than one shop for the sale of pins except on the eve of the New Year and New Year's Day, when it was customary for women to receive presents of pins or the money with which to buy them. In this country it became the practice for merchants and other tradesmen, who had concluded a satisfactory bargain, to give something towards the purchase of pins for the wife or daughter of the person with whom the bargain was struck. This gave rise to the term 'pin money' for the sum allotted to a woman for personal expenses which would include the cost of the many pins needed for the making and the fastening of her dresses.

Although the French held the pin trade until the early 17th century, English pins had already begun to gain a reputation for their quality. In 1650, Ralph Verney, writing from France, was anxious that his wife should be provided with 'proper pinns' from London for, he stated, 'they are nought here'.

While every well-dressed woman had an ample supply of pins for dressing-table use, she also carried about with her a small emergency supply to remedy any mishap to her dress, a fact which on one occasion Samuel Pepys had good reason to note. On August 18th, 1666, he wrote: 'Turned into St Dunstan's Church, where I heard an able sermon of the minister of the place; and stood by a pretty, modest maid, whom I did labour to take by the hand, but she would not, but got further from me; and at last I could perceive her to take pins out of her pocket to prick me if I should touch her again—which seeing I did forbear, and was glad I did spy her design.'

Such pins were often carried in small cylindrical cases known as pincushion boxes or pin-poppets, fashioned from solid ivory and even mounted with gold and enamel. The interior, little more than half an inch in diameter, is fitted with a stuffed pad of velvet or satin, into which a dozen or so pins could be stuck (Plate 61). The ivory pin-poppet, of somewhat later date, on the extreme right of this illustration, was almost certainly made as a betrothal gift, as it has a pattern of two hearts aflame on one side and the representation of a church on the cover.

Many 17th- and 18th-century pincushions were made from material salvaged from embroidered waistcoats, brocaded gold and silver gowns and other articles of clothing (Plate 63), or from scraps cut from a garment worn at some important function and treasured for sentimental reasons. Other were made from pieces obtained from Court dressmakers who had many odd cuttings from the costly stuffs they were always handling, and which they were willing to dispose of to good advantage; a character in Congreve's *Way of the World* remarks: 'Thou art a Retailer of Phrases, and dost deal in Remnants of Remnants like a Maker of Pincushions.'

In Queen Anne's reign there arose a singular fashion for decorating large heart-shaped or rectangular pincushions with pins inserted in such a manner that the heads spelt out a phrase or greeting to mark some notable event either private or national in character (Plate 65); they might be of quilted satin, or of brocade with tasselled corners and ornamented with metal thread and galoon. If the occasion was a marriage or a birth in the royal family an elaborate border with a pattern of hearts and crowns in pins might surround the words 'God Bless the King and Queen' or 'Welcome to the Royal Babe'.

The making and sticking of pincushions for such occasions was an indispensable accomplishment for a needlewoman of the 18th century. In 1729, Mrs Delany (then Mrs Pendarves), in a letter to her sister who lived at Gloucester, wrote: 'Mrs Dashwood junior is as well as can be expected considering her condition; I have got her pincushion to stick for her.' Twelve years later, when her own sister was expecting her first child, Mrs Delany sent her a cushion of quilted satin that she had made for her, but 'as for pins', she wrote, 'I think you must pay the compliment to Gloucester of buying pins there'. This last allusion is, of course, explained by the fact that the pin trade was a well-established industry in Gloucester, where it continued to flourish until the middle of the last century. At Bishop Hooper's Lodging in Westgate Street, a 16th-century house now turned into a Folk Museum, the old pin-maker's workshop with its original forge may still be seen on the top storey, while on the outside of the building is the ladder by which the workpeople had to climb to their work.

Meanwhile, the London pinners were becoming renowned for their fine pointing and polishing. Their reputation for work of high quality may be judged from the following advertisement which appeared in a Birmingham newspaper in 1753:

'This is to give notice, That at the Pin Warehouse in Corbett's Lane, in the High Street, Birmingham, are to be sold Joseph Allen's best London Pins, as good as are produced by any in the Trade, and as cheap as in London   by John Allen, Peruke Maker.'

It was now reckoned that from start to finish it took more than twenty persons to make a pin, the separation of the various processes resulting not only in speedier production but more reliable workmanship. Yet, in spite of the passing of the centuries, no substitute had been found for the coiled wire head. The greatest advance in methods of manufacture had come in the 16th century with the introduction into general use of the steel draw-plate with its graduated series of holes through which the wire could be drawn to any gauge, as required, thus permitting the standardisation of the size of pins, most of which at this time were made of brass.

Plate 60 is a reproduction of a woodcut depicting the interior of a pinner's workshop in the 18th century. In the background is a workman at the draw-bench, and at the end of this, a revolving cage on to which the wire was wound. When it had been reduced to the correct thickness, the wire was straightened by passing it between a double row of nails driven upright into the bench with just enough space to allow the wire to be pulled forcibly through them; only the end nails of the two rows were placed opposite, the rest being alternated on either side. The wire was next cut into lengths equal to six pins and passed to the pointers, who ground both ends of each piece to a point, cut off two pins, and repeated the process until all six had been sharpened.

The task of fitting on the heads was allotted to young children, whose small fingers were best suited to handling the fine coils of wire. They sat at a table with a tray of the heads in front of them, and, thrusting each pin into the heap, picked up a head on the point and slid it along to the blunt end. The woman depicted in the woodcut is seated at a primitive drop-stamp and is striking the heads between two dies, thus fixing them in position and, at the same time, forming them into a round ball. To prevent danger from pricking, brass pins were blanched—that is, given a coating of tin, by boiling them for several hours with granular tin in a solution of lees of wine. Finally, they were thrown into a rotating barrel with bran, for drying and polishing, the bran later being blown away by a method similar to the winnowing of corn.

By George I's reign the itinerant pin-seller, with his box under one arm and a long paper of pins in his hand, was already a familiar figure in the London streets, his cry of 'Pretty maids, Pretty Pins, Pretty Women' bringing many customers hurrying to their doors (Fig. 6). It was the comparative ease with which pins could now be obtained that prompted the needlewomen of the period to construct endless varieties of pincushions from every kind of material. With the vogue for fine silk knitting, pin-balls had come into fashion, made in two pieces joined together with braid or stitching and stuffed with cotton-wool (Plate 62). They were worn swinging from the waist on ribbons or lucetted cords; many had a date and initials combined with the decorative knitting. Pincushions embroidered with political or patriotic slogans were also made, the latter being especially popular among followers of Bonnie Prince Charlie.

Others, smaller and more delicately stitched, were worked with pious sentiments and verses of a religious nature, inspired by the writings of John and Charles Wesley and, one suspects, were designed not so much for use as to display the skill, patience and highmindedness of the person who made them. On the round cushion in Plate 64, only one and a half inches in diameter, the lettering is so fine that the cross-stitching is barely visible; the embroidress has here taken the unusual precaution of protecting her work by covering it with glass.

Another type of small cushion, which was suspended from the waist, was composed of two pieces of ivory, often elaborately carved or pierced, with a flat cushion between them, to which they were attached by stitching; a silk ribbon, surrounding the edge of the cushion, was extended to provide a long loop for suspension at the waist. Three of these are illustrated in the bottom row of Plate 66; one has its original long loop, the other two have shortened ribbons, to make them more suitable for use in a work-box.

Fig. 6. 'Pretty maids, pretty pins, pretty women', from an old woodcut of London Cries.

In spite of the obvious objections to their use, pins still played an important part in the arrangement of a woman's dress, indeed, many years had yet to pass before less dangerous appliances such as hooks and eyes and safety pins were produced commercially in quantity and at reasonable prices. William Hone, who was born in 1780, recalls that when he was a child the raucous voices of women pin-sellers were often to be heard crying:

> *Three rows a penny, Pins;*
> *Shorts, Whites and Mid-dl-ings!*

while girls and women came running into the street to replenish their small stocks. In complete contrast we find, in 1797, an Archduchess of the Austrian

Court, Marie Clémentine, a niece of the ill-fated Marie Antoinette, ordering no fewer than 108 packets of pins for her trousseau.

Much of the fine stitching that had formerly been devoted to the embroidery of samplers was at this time employed in the making of pincushions, some of them of neatly sewn patchwork, the seams stuck with pins little more than half an inch in length. Many of the smallest of these cushions were filled with emery powder and were intended for polishing rusty needles (Plate 67); they can usually be distinguished from the diminutive pincushions of the period by their weight. A red silk strawberry or a small cushion set in a vase of imitation ivory may be filled with either emery or cotton-wool. These are the toys of needlework, made in the form of everyday objects to be played with, wondered at and admired. In some instances the shape of the object was cut in duplicate from thin layers of ivory or shell, and a flat, silk-covered cushion pressed between them. A miniature coach, a wheelbarrow, a book or a pair of bellows are often to be found. Alternatively, two pieces of card would be cut out, covered with silk and stitched firmly round the edges, the pins being inserted at intervals between the two layers. An embroidered fan, a shoe, a painted silk fish with pins for fins might all be made in this manner; nothing was too fanciful for these engaging trifles (Plate 68).

Towards the end of the Georgian era a London manufacturer, of Paternoster Row, began to make cushions of this type with picturesque views or buildings of historical interest, printed on silk, to be sold as souvenirs at fashionable watering places. One example, which may be seen in Plate 69, has on one side a map of the Isle of Wight and on the other a picture of East Cowes Castle. In 1827 the death of Frederick, Duke of York, was commemorated by a similar cushion with his portrait and a eulogistic account of his life, in particular of his work which earned for him the title of 'The Soldier's Friend'. Inserted round this cushion are mourning pins made from iron and coated with black enamel.

In construction, the domestic pin at this date remained basically the same as it had been for several centuries, that is to say it was still composed of two separate pieces of wire. Continuous experiments over the years had brought about improvements in the techniques of production: about 1800 a manufacturer of Gracechurch Street, London, announced that he had adopted a new method 'for putting on the heads of this very useful little article with greater expedition and uniformity than has been previously done by others'— a uniformity that was obtained by the use of a machine of much greater precision than the primitive drop-stamp previously employed in the industry. The white layette pincushion in Plate 70, dating from about 1820, has been stuck with a large number of these new pins, the neat, smooth heads of which would have astonished Mrs Delany and her friends; but on close inspection the coiled wire of the head can still be distinguished. The miniature sampler in Plate 64, made in the year of Queen Victoria's accession, is still stuck with the old wire-headed pins. Within a few years, however, D. F. Tayler and Co., 'Manufacturers to Queen Victoria and all the Royal Family', were producing long papers of pins on which was printed the following advertisement:

'The inimitable patent Solid Headed Pins exclusively made by D. F. Tayler and Co., London, on a new and improved principle, are unlike those of any other manufacture in consequence of the whole pin being formed of one piece of wire whereby the head is rendered immovable and its slipping off is impossible.'

The modern pin, cheap and reliable, had, at last, become generally available.

The Victorian age abounded with pincushions: the crinolined doll, its flounced skirts amply stuck with glass-headed and ordinary pins; the large pumpkin-shaped cushion encircled with overlapping tiers of ribbon, lace or crochet; the small silver models of birds and animals with blue velvet cushions inset in their backs; the beribboned monstrosities hollowed out in the centre to contain a flower vase or a scent bottle.

To describe more than a few would take many pages. There is nevertheless a notable example of a commemorative pincushion that deserves special mention. It was made in patchwork in the diamond jubilee year of 1897, and might occasionally be seen standing on the table of an Edwardian drawing-room. Elaborately built up of cardboard in the form of a many-pointed star, it was composed of sixty diamond facets to commemorate the 'sixty glorious years' of Queen Victoria's reign. Many of these cushions were made by needlewomen very little, if any, younger than the Sovereign whose accession they so well remembered; but though of a comparatively late date, the careful seaming of the patches with their almost invisible stitching is typical of a much earlier age; of the days, that is, when a pincushion was not merely a receptacle for holding pins, but a family treasure, an emblem, or even an heirloom.

6

Needlework Clamps

UNTIL the middle of the 19th century sewing with the aid of a clamp was still a common practice in this country. The main purpose of such an implement was to fix one end of a piece of material firmly to a table so that the seamstress could hold it taut with one hand while stitching with the other. In the days when nearly all clothing was made in the home, and there were long hems of sheets and other household linen to be sewn by hand, the employment of a device of this kind was of considerable importance if the work was to be done smoothly and efficiently.

But though the use to which these clamps were put was prosaic enough, their construction could show great originality of design. Like other articles of domestic use they were frequently given as presents and, as preparations for a marriage in earlier centuries usually involved many months of sewing, they were sometimes, very appropriately, offered as love-tokens. The 17th-century clamp illustrated in Plate 72 was certainly designed as a gift of this kind. It is constructed of wood veneered with bone backed by metal foil, the main decoration on the front panel being two hearts aflame. In addition to the reels on either side for holding thread, there are interior compartments for needles and thimble.

Another clamp made as a token of affection is illustrated in Plate 73. It is carved from morse ivory and dates from the early years of Queen Anne's reign. Here the kneeling swain offers his heart in the form of a pincushion which he bears on his head; his wig, extending horizontally backwards, merges into the shape of a dog's head—symbolising the faithful hound that he would no doubt like to emulate.

By the end of the 18th century it is evident that sewing clamps existed in considerable quantities, though their distribution was uneven. As with many other objects of this kind they might be readily obtainable in the London shops, and at the more exclusive resorts such as Bath or Tunbridge Wells, which catered for the fashionable world, but were little known elsewhere. Parson Woodforde records in his Diary on February 8th, 1793, that 'Mrs Custance sent Nancy by Mr Custance a small present of Tunbridge Ware, a sort of Vice with a Cushion to pin work to a Table'. From the wording of his entry it is clear that in the small Norfolk parish in which the Woodfordes lived a sewing clamp, even at this period, was still something of a curiosity.

For ordinary household sewing the type of clamp most generally used in Georgian times was circular or rectangular in shape, of ivory or wood, and surmounted by a vase-like receptacle supporting a pincushion. Even here, however, there was a great variety in both size and detail. The large wooden clamp on the right of Plate 74, for instance, has a removable lid with a mirror inset on the underside, the hollow cup being intended to hold thimble or wax. The cylindrical clamp on the left of the same illustration also has a top that can be removed and an interior compartment for holding powdered alum or French chalk to sprinkle on the hands during long hours of hemming—a necessary precaution to prevent the staining of the material or the rusting of the needle.

Another simple and particularly efficient type of implement is the squat, rectangular clamp, usually known as a box clamp (Plate 74). The broad top ensured a firm grip of linen and other stout materials while at the same time providing a suitable platform for a pincushion to which more delicate fabrics could be secured with a pin if desired. The square front also lent itself conveniently to decoration, and, when of ivory, was sometimes carved in the form of a flower. The example second from the left in Plate 74 was probably made for, or possibly by, the donor as a gift of special importance, for it is carefully carved from wood and inlaid with ivory and shell, not merely on the outside, but also on the inner surfaces which are visible only when the clamp is not in use. Large wooden clamps of this type were sometimes surmounted by a drawer in which oddments for sewing could be kept, and when of Continental origin were painted in patterns of bright colours.

Until the early part of the last century silk, linen and cotton thread, as well as wool, was wound by the manufacturers into skeins, and was obtained in this form from the shops. Before use it had to be transferred on to spools, reels or flat winders of various kinds (see Chapter 2). Finding someone to hold the thread was not always an easy matter, indeed in a busy household a pair of hands could ill be spared for so simple a task. Special clamps were made, therefore, of wood, ivory or metal, supporting a hollow winding frame or cradle revolving on a spindle and sometimes surmounted by a shallow cup in which the ball could rest; they were used in pairs, the skein of thread being stretched between them (Plate 78). For wool-winding the cradle might be from three to four inches in depth, but those used for linen and cotton thread were much smaller.

When, towards the end of the Georgian era, manufacturers began to sell their sewing thread wound ready for use, either in balls or on wooden reels, these clamps were no longer needed. They were not, however, entirely discarded, as they could always be used for hemming, if so required. It is for this reason that an odd winding clamp may often be found in an old work-box, whereas pairs are now relatively uncommon.

Many hemming clamps are surmounted by a spindle and a small reel for holding sewing thread. In front of the reel there may also be a carved knob over which a foundation loop for netting could be slipped—a more convenient device than the older, lead-weighted cushion (Plates 75 and 79). In the fitted work-boxes of late Georgian days tubular cases of bone or ivory containing netting shuttles and gauges are sometimes accompanied by netting clamps carved to match. During the latter part of the 18th century the steel toymakers of Sheffield, Birmingham and Wolverhampton began to turn their attention to the manufacture of sewing clamps of various kinds. Some were provided with a pincushion, others, intended for netting only, terminated in a simple hook or knob. They were light to handle, and could be elegant and extremely decorative with their many sparkling facets, those of the more costly type having their own satin and velvet lined cases (Plate 80). Winding clamps made from metal are less common, but an exceptionally fine pair of French 18th-century steel clamps with flat chased decoration, used for wool-winding, may be seen in Plate 77.

Victorian sewing clamps, in keeping with the more staid and practical tastes of the times, were of heavier construction, of either plain or polished wood; or they might be of Tunbridge ware (Plate 76), and were sometimes decorated with small engravings printed or glued on to the surface. Most of them were topped by a pincushion, but, as work-boxes were now in general use, compartments for needles and thimble and elaborate contrivances for holding thread, which were so necessary in earlier days, were no longer required. Also belonging to this period are the clamps used for Macramé or knotted-fringe work; they were made in pairs and may easily be distinguished by the round-topped pegs between which the main cord for supporting the fringe was stretched.

The most ingenious of all sewing clamps, and far less common, is the hemming-bird, an invention of early Georgian days that did not come into general use until the beginning of the 19th century (Plate 81). In this case the clamp itself is of secondary importance; it is surmounted by a metal bird fitted with a strong spring underneath the body and so devised that the beak opens and closes as the tail is depressed and released. The material, when inserted in the bird's mouth, was gripped and firmly held there, with this great advantage—its position could be changed with a simple movement of the hand and without loosening the screw by which the clamp was fixed to the table. Hemming-birds, if of early origin, are often cast in solid bronze, either with or without plumage markings; more delicately modelled birds carrying a spindle or pincushion on their backs, and with a case for needles attached to the lower part of the clamp, occur in the latter part of the 18th century. Those of hollow metal, occasionally made of silver, belong to a later period.

Sewing-birds or 'grippers', as they were generally termed, became extremely popular in the United States at the beginning of the 19th century. Early examples possess an individuality of their own, having been made by hand, in some instances, probably by a local blacksmith; but towards the middle of the century factory-made clamps were being produced in considerable quantities, particularly in Connecticut. Many of them were provided with a hook that could be used for netting and, more especially, for rug-making; they were therefore known as rug-braiders. On the newer clamps models of butterflies, dogs, stags and other objects replaced the more familiar bird.

In 1852 an advertisement appeared in a Connecticut newspaper advising the use of a sewing clamp which, it maintained, would help to ensure an upright and 'health preserving' posture when sewing. About 1830 in this country a number of cast metal hemming clamps were made having a similar spring action and surmounted by dolphins, cupids and other fantastic creations of a most elaborate character (Plate 82). Some of these appeared at the trade exhibitions in the early part of Queen Victoria's reign, but, in fact, their day was already drawing to a close for, with the introduction of the sewing machine, the hand stitching of long seams was becoming unnecessary.

The earliest authenticated accounts of experiments in mechanical sewing occur in the middle of the 18th century: in 1755 Charles Weisenthal took out a patent in England for a machine with a double-pointed needle having an eye at mid-length. Further and more significant progress was made in 1790 when an English cabinet maker, Thomas Saint, patented his improved sewing machine in which several principles that are incorporated in the most modern machines first appeared. This was followed by Barthelemy Thimmonier's chain-stitch machine, in reality a mechanical form of tambouring, a hook being used in place of a needle. Later still, about 1834, Walter Hunt of New

York constructed a lock stitch machine, having a curved needle with an eye in the point.

The greatest advance, however, came in 1846, when another American, Elias Howe, took out a patent for a lock stitch machine which became the forerunner of the sewing machine as we know it today. Though Howe's invention brought him great prosperity in his own country, his affairs did not prosper here, and it was eventually Isaac Singer who, by patenting an improvement to Howe's model, first introduced and then popularised the sewing machine in England.

The task of persuading a sceptical public that such a device was a workable proposition was by no means easy, as many people had been deluded by false claims made for earlier and less satisfactory models. At one period, to convince possible customers of the practical worth of his invention, Singer took his machine from house to house, offering to give demonstrations on people's doorsteps, until, at last having gained the confidence of the public, the success of his venture was assured.

With the introduction of the sewing machine into the home and, what was equally important, the increasing use of mechanical sewing in industry, which brought many things into the shops that had, formerly, to be made laboriously by hand, hemming clamps fell entirely into disuse. Handling some of the more fanciful and delicately made of these implements at the present day it is, indeed, difficult to realise that they were ever intended for very serious use. Yet it is by no means unusual on an old clamp to find four or five layers of worn material concealing the original covering of the pincushion, evidence, if any were needed, of hard and constant use throughout several generations. The needlework clamp was never a mere toy: in earlier centuries it served an important practical purpose.

7

Sewing Caskets, Chatelaines, Work-boxes and Work-tables

IN ANGLO-SAXON ENGLAND women carried their needlework implements in cylindrical metal boxes, about three inches in height and two inches in diameter, suspended from the girdle chain (Plate 85). Specimens have been unearthed showing signs of gilding and other decoration and containing fragments of material as well as needles and thread. In the domestic life of this period and, indeed, for many centuries to come, there was little provision for the safe storage of personal belongings: privacy, as we understand it, was quite unknown. Small individual possessions were therefore, of necessity, carried on the person. Not only sewing implements, but keys, pomander, seal, pen-knife and earspoon, swung from the waist on chains or cords.

These accessories lent themselves naturally to enrichment and decoration and came eventually to be regarded as a symbol of occupation and rank. In a large house or castle, for instance, it became the prerogative of the mistress or chatelaine to wear an elaborate equipage of this kind, and in the course of time the name chatelaine passed from the wearer to the object itself. Embroidered pouches were sometimes used for holding needlework tools (Plate 83) and by the end of the 17th century small caskets and etuis containing a few articles connected with sewing had also made their appearance.

An unusual example, intended for a child, may be seen in Plate 8. It is covered with gold brocaded tissue and lined with pink satin. The clasp with which it is fastened is secured by a large silver pin inserted at the front edge of the lid. Inside are compartments for holding a thimble, a very small pair of scissors, and pins; and it also contains a piece of red cloth into which needles could be stuck, and a page prepared for writing in silverpoint. On this last, written with the silver pin that secures the clasp, is the following pathetic little note: 'My Dear Child Thomas was Born January ye 24th 1734[5] privately Baptised ye 26th and Died ye 19th February and was Beried ye 22nd.'

As by the end of the 17th century silverpoint writing was already becoming outmoded and graphite pencils were in general use, it is probable that the casket had been in the owner's possession when she herself was a child, or had been handed down to her from an even earlier generation. Another elaborately contrived casket of a similarly early date, with Buhl decoration, is illustrated in Plate 86. This also contains a silverpoint writing tablet, backing a mirror, but apart from this and the silk lining of the lid nothing of the original contents remains, the case having been relined and refitted with sewing implements in Victorian times.

In 1714, George Willdey at the Great Toy Shop in Ludgate Street was advertising scissors, needlecase and thimble, attached by short chains to a clasp fitting over the waistbelt. He also stocked huswifes, but a case or box containing a variety of needlework tools was as yet a rarity. This was still the age of the pedlar who bought his stock from individual craftsmen and called with his wares from door to door, and of the provincial fairs where the different tradesmen set up their booths in field or market place. These fairs were of great importance, catering not only for the simpler village folk, but for the wealthier classes who came long distances in their coaches to visit them.

At the famous Stourbridge Fair, held each September in a cornfield two miles from Cambridge, and said to be the largest in Europe, the shops or booths were built in rows like streets, with covered walks down which women of fashion could stroll at their leisure, inspecting the stalls of the mercers, the glovers, the silversmiths, the toy-sellers and the lacemen, to see what new and extravagant trifles they had to offer. At one stall they might find a delicately spun gold thimble in a shagreen case; at another, a pair of fine Sheffield scissors; and at another, a needlecase of mother-of-pearl, brought, perhaps, from France.

To have assembled a number of such objects for sale in a single container with specially shaped compartments would have required a degree of co-operation among the various craftsmen that was far in advance of the general practices of the times. The exceptions were the large and costly fitted cases that were given as presents in royal circles on the occasion of a marriage or some other important event. But these were in no sense work-boxes; they contained a large number of toilet requisites and were intended for dressing-table use.

In some 17th- and 18th-century paintings, particularly in the more homely domestic scenes, wooden boxes may be seen with the lid padded on the outside and stuck with pins or needles (Plate 158). Much larger cushion-shaped boxes are also depicted, with rounded and padded tops covered with brocade or some coloured, striped material, stretched most probably over a wicker framework (Plates 185 and 23). These were the forerunners of the modern work-box, but were without fittings, being used mainly to hold skeins of wool and silk and sometimes the work itself. Shallow bowl-shaped baskets were employed for a similar purpose and frequently appear in contemporary portraits. In 1756, Ann Stanhope, writing to her brother of the adventures of a mischievous puppy, says: 'I was working a beautiful Apron and he has tore it all to pieces; and steals things out of my work Baskett.'

A needlework casket dating from the mid-18th century made in the form of a cottage may be seen in Plate 84. It is of ivory and contains sewing tools of silver. Such caskets are, however, extremely rare. The type of case most generally used at this period, among those who could afford so expensive a possession, was an upright etui, oval in section, about five inches in height, and tapering slightly towards the base (Plate 88). It might be of enamel, silver or silver-gilt, or covered with shagreen or leather of various colours. It invariably contained a bodkin and a pair of folding scissors and occasionally a case for needles, while there were also numerous objects of everyday use such as a knife and fork screwing into silver handles, a toothpick, an ear-spoon, a buttonhook, a pen, a rule and a pair of compasses, all ingeniously contrived to fit into their separate compartments. In this instance the problem of assembling such a diversity of objects presented little difficulty as they were all the work of the cutler or silversmith and few different processes and materials were involved.

Later in the century embroidered and quilted pouches of various kinds, containing similar sets of implements, came into fashion. Mrs Rea, waiting-woman to Mrs Delany, in a letter written in 1779, gives the following description of a pouch of this kind that had just been given to her mistress by Queen Charlotte: 'It was a *most beautiful* pocket case, the outside white sattin work'd with gold, and ornamented with gold spangles; . . . it is lined with pink sattin, and contains a knife, sizsars, pencle, rule, compas and bodkin, and more than I can say; but it is all gold and mother-of-pearl. At one end there was a little letter case that contained a letter directed to Mrs Delany written in the Queen's own hand.'

Here, again, it will be seen that there are only a few sewing tools; a woman still carried her needlework accessories in the deep and roomy pockets concealed in the folds of her dress, or in a large embroidered bag that accompanied her on social occasions, a fashion that continued until the last years of the 18th century when there was a marked change in feminine attire. The full skirts with their ample folds were suddenly replaced by the slim, high-waisted

43. Thread waxers with ivory and mother-of-pearl mounts. The yard measure in the top row has a cake of white wax beneath. The two cakes of beeswax in the bottom row are decorated with gold paper.

44. (*above*) Wax box with lathe decoration; large wooden cotton barrel; lead weight, with Tunbridge ware top and base, for steadying material while working. (*below*) Wooden box, in the form of a lemon, holding wax; small horn embroidery frame; china darning egg.

45. Victorian work-box, walnut with bronze mounts; (*in front*) a wooden wool bowl, and three darning eggs made from horn, Tunbridge ware, and an immature coconut.

46. (*left to right*) Needle-case with shell veneer; peach stone powder sprinkler: ivory needle-case; scent bottle in ivory case; silver filigree case for wax, thimble and yard measure. (*in front*) Silver scent bottle, and ivory powder sprinkler.

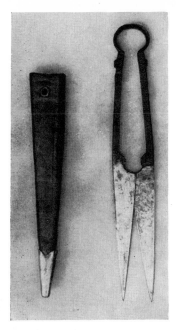
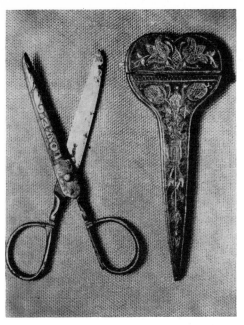
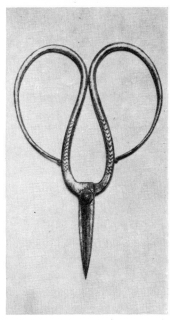

47. Spring scissors with metal-tipped leather sheath; 17th century. 48. English 17th-century scissors engraved 'love' and 'dieu' on the cut. Iron scissor case, engraved and gilt; German, 17th century. 49. Chinese snipping scissors with welded steel cutting edges.

50. Ivory-handled seam knife. Steel scissors with crown handle, and shank in form of crucifix with etched figure. 51. Scissors: English, with silver handles and sheath; Spanish, with etched decoration on steel; German, with cast bronze handles and sheath. (*below*) Persian scissors, with brass handles and deeply hollowed steel blades damascened with gold.

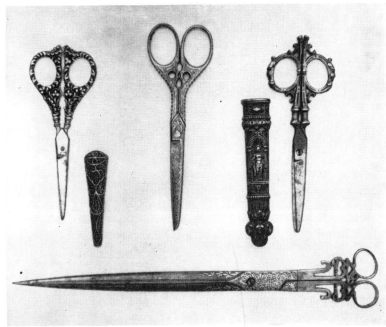

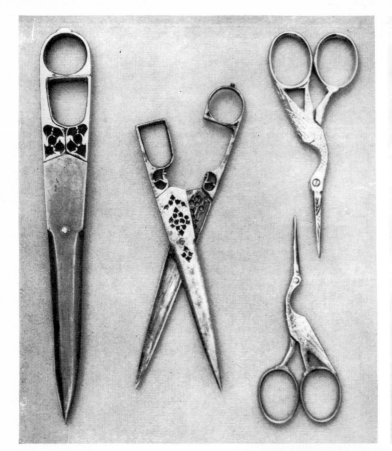

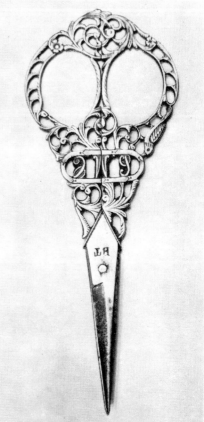

52. Persian steel scissors with hollowed blades and pierced decoration. Spanish and French stork scissors.

53. Italian scissors of finely pierced steel.

54. (*left*) Scissors with elaborately ornamented handles and sheath, and (*right*) with gold handles and chased gold sheath; *c.* 1800. (*centre*) Small French scissors with silver handles; *c.* 1710.

55. Madonna sewing, with spring scissors in open basket; School of Bruges; *c.* 1520. From a series of miniatures.

56. French pearl-handled scissors with gold mounts.

57. Scissor case of brocaded material; and sweet bag in the form of a pod, of silk with gold braid. Both have loops for suspension from the waist.

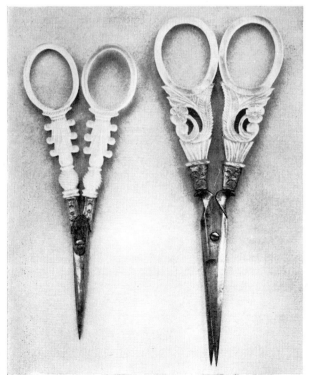

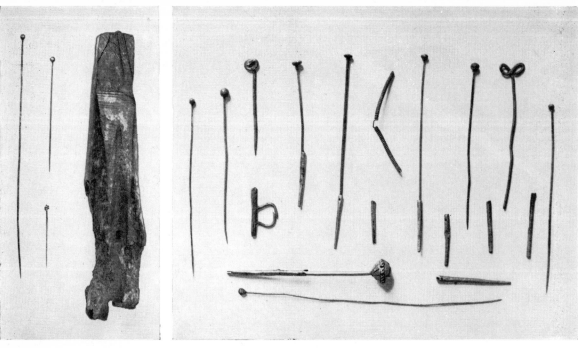

58. Two medieval dress pins, and one household pin, of bronze; (*right*) a pinner's bone. 59. Early bronze pins and point protectors; in the centre, a length of coiled wire for making pin-heads.

60. Pin-maker's workshop in the 18th century, with girl fixing pin-heads with a primitive drop stamp. 61. Ivory pin-poppets; 17th and 18th centuries. 62. Pin-balls knitted in coloured silks and made to swing from the waist.

63. English early
17th-century
pincushion, silk and
silver thread on
linen, mainly tent
stitch.

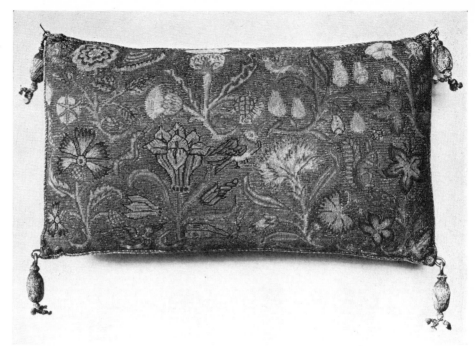

64. Embroidered silk pincushions; *c.* 1770. Sampler pincushion, $2\frac{1}{4}'' \times 1\frac{1}{4}''$; 1837.   65. Layette pincushion
stuck with large coiled-headed pins; early 18th century.

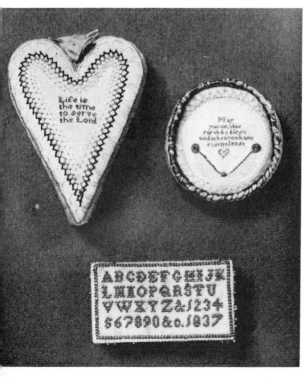

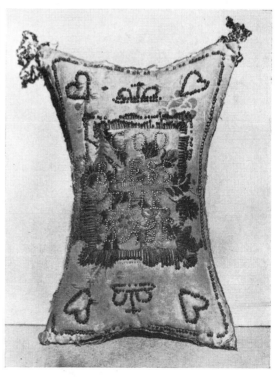

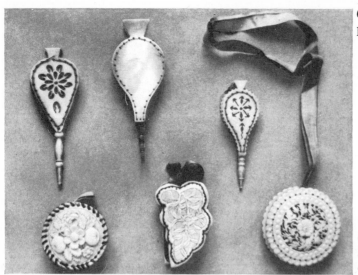

66. Ivory and mother-of-pearl pincushions; 18th and 19th centuries.

67. Emery cushions of various materials, and two patchwork pin-balls; early 19th century.

68. Small early 19th-century pin-cushions, (*left*) hand-painted silk with metal mount; (*centre*) patchwork; (*right*) bark with quill embroidery. (*below*) Early Victorian painted silk cushion.

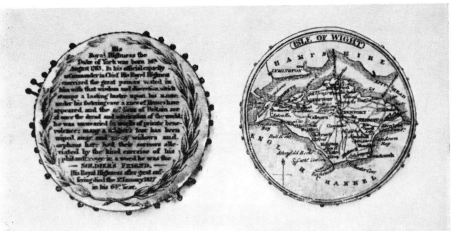

69. Printed silk disc pincushions, (*left*) stuck with black pins in memory of the Dule of York, 1827; (*right*) with map of the Isle of Wight, and engraving of Cowes Castle on reverse.

70. Layette pincushion; early 19th century.

71. Embroidered material at some period made into a pincushion, but found, on unpicking, to have been a woman's coif of the later 16th century.

72. Wooden sewing clamp veneered with bone, made as a love token. In addition to the two movable reels, there are interior compartments for needles and thimble; 17th century.

73. Early 18th-century clamp of morse ivory, made as a betrothal offering.

74. Two turned wooden sewing clamps with vase tops; early 19th century. *(centre)* Box clamp, wood inlaid with ivory; and steel clamp with applied metal decoration; 18th century.

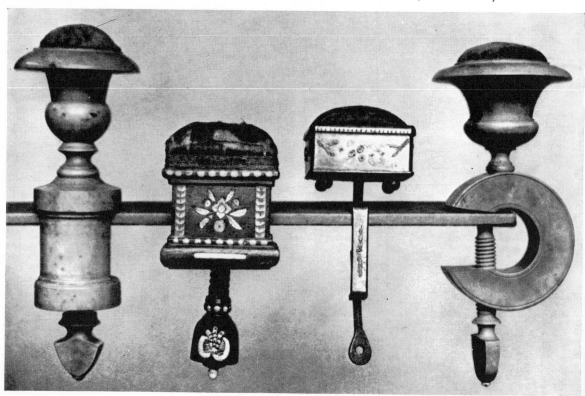

75. Ivory clamps of the 18th and 19th centuries; the second and fifth could be used for netting.

76. Tunbridge ware sewing clamp. 77. Pair of French steel wool-winding clamps, with flat chased decoration, overall height 1 ft.; 18th century.

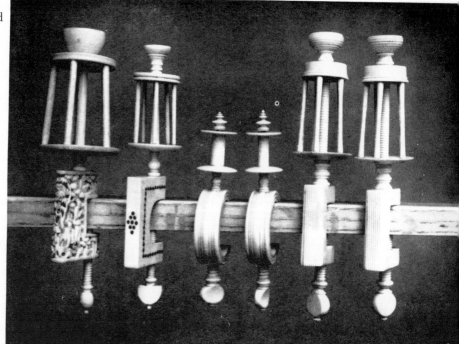

78. Two odd ivory winding clamps and two pairs; 18th century.

79. Clamps of wood, steel and ivory, having a knob or hook for use in netting. (*below*) Lead-weighted cushion for netting or macramé.

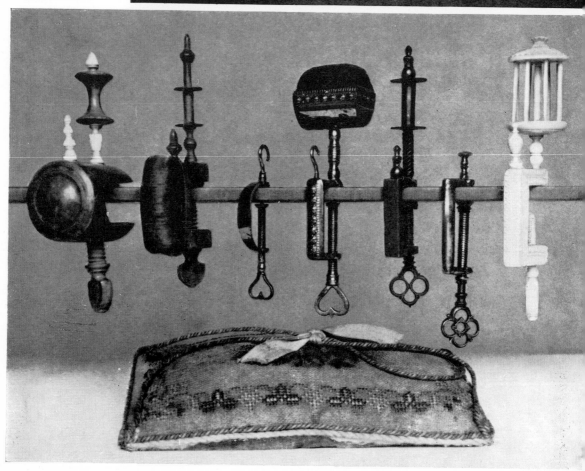

o. Fine cut-steel netting clamp in velvet-
ned leather case; late 18th century.

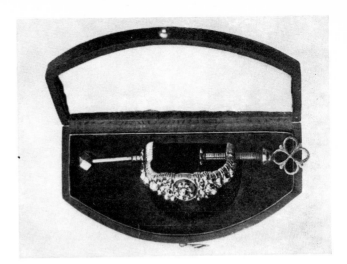

81. Bronze hemming-birds; c.
1800.

82. Cast metal sewing clamps, 1820–1840.
The mouth of the fish opens to grasp the
material when the tail is depressed. The foot
of the cupid holds the material, lifting up
when pressure is put on the wings.

83. Small embroidered pouch for needlework tools; 17th century.　84. Ivory needlework casket with silver fittings; mid 18th century.

85. Anglo-Saxon bronze sewing box, worn suspended from the girdle.

86. Buhl sewing casket, c. 1690. The interior was relined and refitted in the Victorian era. (Closed and open.)

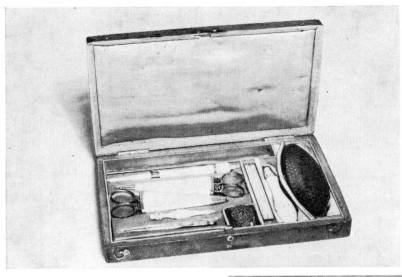

87. Late 18th-century work-box covered with shagreen.

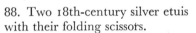

88. Two 18th-century silver etuis with their folding scissors.

89. Black lacquered box decorated with studs of burnished steel, the lid set with a large shell carved to represent Venus and Cupid in a chariot. In the base is a musical box playing two tunes; the tray contains fittings of mother-of-pearl with gold mounts; *c.* 1800.

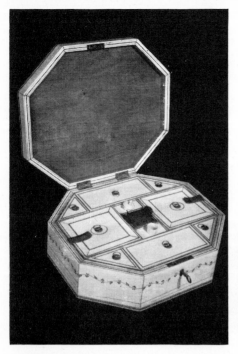

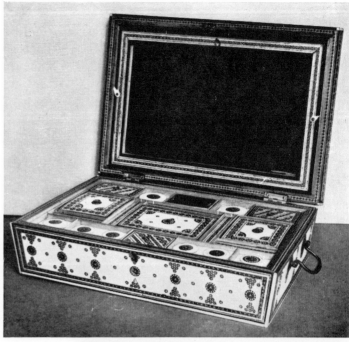

90. Octagonal box, ivory over sandalwood; Madras, 1790.

91. Indian work-box of inlaid ivory veneer with cotton barrels and numerous compartments; late 18th century.

92. (Right) Spinet box with gilt feet and ornaments and fittings of pearl. It contains a musical-box playing two tunes; Paris. *c.* 1800.

93. (Below) Ivory box, with silver feet and handles; Madras, 1790.

dresses of the Directoire period, and the capacious pockets, in consequence, disappeared.

For a time, the embroidered bags were made even larger to hold the numberless small articles they now had to carry; but for sewing implements in everyday domestic use it was soon found that some more practical receptacle was required. It was to meet this necessity that, at long last, the work-box as we know it today came into being. Divided into many compartments, and with matching sets of implements in silver, ivory or pearl, that advancements in industry were now making more readily available, it satisfied so genuine a need that its development was as rapid as it was varied.

By the turn of the century work-boxes were being produced in all shapes and sizes and in materials of every description. Some of the finest examples at this period were made in India and China for the large numbers of Europeans visiting or residing in those countries (Plates 90, 91 and 93). Ivory caskets on gilded feet; lacquered chests; coffers of sandalwood; trunks, in miniature, covered with leather or galuchat; boxes of tortoiseshell, or with fine inlay of amboyna and all the rich and varied woods of the East, were produced in endless variety. In the early part of the last century large, lacquered work-boxes, containing sets of carved implements, were on sale at many Eastern seaports, where they were bought by sailors to take home to their wives and sweethearts (Plate 96). The name of the recipient was painted, to order, inside the lid, and the fittings could be supplied in bone or ivory according to the purchaser's means.

It may be noticed that in some Eastern work-boxes the implements show no signs of having been used and, in contrast to the carefully carved and inlaid containers, the fittings are often hastily and faultily made. The reason for this is that to the native workmen the construction and decoration of the box was an age-old craft carried out with meticulous care and devotion, while the fittings, copied from specimens sent out from Europe, were unfamiliar and their exact purpose little understood. A cotton barrel may therefore be found without an interior spindle or a hole through which the thread can be drawn; a horizontal winder intended for netting may be without its ratchet, and a netting needle provided with an 'eye' at each end and with the tips unslit.

Boxes of English workmanship were constructed from many kinds of woods and from materials as diverse as papier-mâché and alabaster; the implements they contained were equally varied—from pinchbeck to gold encrusted with pearls. As many were intended for betrothal or wedding gifts a panel or shield was often provided for a name, a date, or a coat of arms. Brass-bound trunks covered in velvet contained a tray of sewing tools with spaces for quills, ink and pounce pots beneath. A miniature chest of drawers might be filled with both sewing and writing materials. In the early part of the 19th century basket-shaped sewing-boxes were much in vogue, the double lid divided and hinged in the centre (Plate 100).

A very remarkable Irish work-box of birchwood, with finely executed pen-and-ink decoration, is illustrated in Plate 94; the ornamentation differs from most work of this type as it is tinted. The box was made about 1820 for John Taylor of Tyrone, as a present for his fiancée. The leading figure on horseback is probably John Taylor himself; the name on the signpost possibly that of his estate. His race-horses appear on the cover, with a sporting trophy and fox's mask amid the border of shamrock and roses, while on the side panels are his greyhounds and other subjects connected with country sports; the names of the horses and hounds, in minute lettering, are discernible among the grass. The artist is not known, but he signs himself 'W'.

Another very fine box of a similar date, in light tortoiseshell, and elaborately fitted for needlework and writing, may be seen in Plate 95. The silver inkpots bear the hallmark of 1810. There are two secret drawers; in one of them is a small piece of paper on which is written: 'To my dearest Ann from her own brother Tom'.

It is in the drawers of these work-boxes that one sometimes finds a metal template with a quantity of old cards and letters to be cut up for patchwork. Elizabeth Grant recalls how, when staying at University College, Oxford, in 1810, with her uncle Dr James Griffith, his wife Mary always had a pair of scissors and a pile of old letters and papers beside her; and how Mr Rowley, the Dean, had drawn for her, with a great array of compasses, a small hexagon 'which she had had executed in tin, and from this pattern she cut up all these papers, sitting between dinner and tea, while my uncle finished his port wine'. As the supply of paper in former centuries was limited, there was a constant demand for old letters and documents for use in various forms of needlework; we have it on good authority that it was only by a fortunate chance that Evelyn's Diary was not cut to pieces to make dress patterns.

Delicate straw-work boxes came from France and Italy, and they were among the objects made and sold in this country by French prisoners at the time of the Napoleonic wars. From France and Italy also came the neatly contrived velvet-lined boxes of mahogany and walnut made in the form of spinets, with a mirror inside the lid, sunk compartments to hold the fittings and a musical box in the interior playing two or more tunes (Plate 92). The work-box of the early 19th century was no longer a mere container; it had become an object of significance to be exhibited, wondered at, and admired.

In this connection the following quotation from Hans Andersen's novel *O.T.*, written in 1836, may be of some interest. His heroine, Sophie, while paying a visit to some friends, is told of a valued possession that is about to be shown to her, which belongs to the Mam'selle of the household:

'You will see her little sewing-box with all its curiosities. This little box plays an important part. She takes it with her when she pays visits and it is used to make conversation. Every piece is looked at and handed round ... A wheelbarrow with a pincushion in it; a silver fish containing lavender water; a measure made from silk ribbon; and a small Napoleon of cast-iron.'

The character of Sophie is said to have been drawn from Andersen's first love, whom he never married, and the work-box he described was, no doubt, one that he had actually seen in his younger days. Scent-bottles such as the silver fish are frequently found in old work-boxes (Plate 46), while the cast-iron Napoleon would almost certainly be a standing needle-case of the type referred to in Chapter 1.

In the absence of any more definite clue the approximate age of a box may best be gauged by the provision made for sewing thread. Early examples contain flat winders and barrels; cotton balls appeared about 1805 and remained in use until the Victorian era; reels and reel holders belong to the middle and later part of the century (see Chapter 2). There is, however, a considerable overlapping in these periods; changes took place much less rapidly than they do today. In addition, alterations in the basic shape of a box involved much work and expense so that designs once established were not lightly discarded. Two work-boxes, identical in outward appearance, may have fittings of different periods, the gap in some cases being as much as twenty or thirty years.

Work-tables came into use in the late 18th century, and at this period were made without fittings; they were in the main small, elegant tables, often with lyre supports, and with one, or perhaps two, shallow drawers divided into compartments. The next step was the provision of a silk pouch which hung down beneath the table top, for holding work, skeins of thread and other oddments. Globe-shaped work-stands, the upper half revolving as a lid, also provided accommodation for needlework, but these are more rare. Many of the elaborately made games-tables that were in fashion during the 18th and early 19th centuries were adapted for sewing. In the example illustrated in Plate 102, which has a folding top inlaid for playing chess, backgammon and cribbage, the drawer originally intended for cards, counters and other accessories has been divided to take cotton barrels and similar small objects, a deeper drawer, reminiscent of the earlier silk pouch, pulling out from beneath.

Early 19th-century work-tables were sometimes made in the form of a box mounted on a pedestal with three or four splaying feet, closely resembling, indeed probably converted from, the once familiar tea-poy; more unusual is the neatly contrived work-table with a work-box of matching wood at a lower level (Plate 101).

The typical early Victorian work-table had an octagonal hinged top opening to reveal a tray for accessories which, when lifted out, disclosed a hollow, central well, tapering to the base, and providing ample room for needlework (Plate 103). A small number of these tables were of satinwood, but the majority were of walnut, maple or mahogany, with pie-crust edging. Papier-mâché, which was at this time reaching the height of its popularity, was also used, shell decoration now being added to the painting and gilding of former years. In Birmingham and Wolverhampton, which were celebrated for this type of ware, many elaborate work-tables were produced, their compartments lined with coloured papers and fitted with reel-holders and other accessories of mother-of-pearl.

Meanwhile, for more occasional use, flat cases of sewing implements that could be slipped easily into a beribboned work-bag were being made. In William IV's reign it was still customary for a woman to take her needlework with her when invited to assemblies or private social gatherings. If cards were played a number of tables were set aside round which those who preferred to occupy themselves with sewing and embroidery could sit and talk together. In January, 1832, Lady Wharncliffe, describing a dinner she had attended at the Pavilion at Brighton, wrote to her daughter: 'The evening pass'd very pleasantly at Commerce, which the King seem'd to be amused with', while Queen Adelaide, she continues, 'sat down to work when the King sat down to cards, & was very busy counting the stitches of a *Berlin pattern*, but talking to the Ladies sitting round the table with her.'

In such circumstances the cases carried might be of carved ivory, with fittings of gold or silver-gilt resting in sunk compartments (Plate 98). Or they might be composed of different coloured woods, lined with velvet and with a mirror inside the lid. The example shown in Plate 104 is veneered to represent a barrel, and contains a tambour hook as well as the more ordinary tools. The scent bottle remains; but the writing implements, the ear-spoon, tweezers and other toilet accessories are no longer included, though they are sometimes to be found accompanying scissors and thimble in the many *nécessaires* and fitted leather cases that were made during the Victorian era, intended for use when travelling.

The return to fashion of the full skirt, with its more normal waist-line, had brought the chatelaine back again into favour. Unlike its earlier counterpart this was now composed solely of sewing implements, in matching sets, suspended on long chains (Plate 106). Though of comparatively inexpensive materials, at their best these equipages could be extremely decorative. Those dating from the beginning of the century made of finely cut steel, their diamond facets sparkling with the rippling movements of the skirt, were hardly less ornamental than their more costly predecessors.

The large, pierced or engraved clasp that clipped over the waist belt was as important as the tools themselves; indeed it is probable that many sewing chatelaines were worn for effect rather than for use. They remained in fashion for more than fifty years, though becoming heavier and less pleasing in design, fabricated from ivory, bone and pinchbeck, or sometimes from jet for mourning wear, the thimble still resting in a miniature bucket, the pincushion in the shape of the familiar acorn.

In Edwardian times, long after the chatelaines had been lain aside, these small toys, detached from their chains, were transferred to work-boxes containing the more practical tools that were now coming into very general use and by which they were soon to be replaced. Within little more than a decade ornamentation had virtually disappeared. Opportunities for higher education had resulted in a widening of feminine interests. At the same time, clothing and many household articles, which had formerly been sewn by hand in the home, were now easily obtainable at the shops, thus providing leisure for more varied pursuits. A sewing-box was no longer the centre of a woman's life. Pincushions and needle-cases were needed for use, and not to be handed round 'to make conversation' as they were in the days of Hans Andersen's Mam'selle.

8

Knitting

EXAMPLES of clothing found in Coptic tombs indicate that fine knitting was a well-established art in the 4th and 5th centuries. The Arabs, who were expert knitters, used the process for making carpets and wall-hangings, and it is probable that it was the Arab traders, travelling from country to country, who first taught the peoples of the Mediterranean lands to knit, the knowledge of the craft spreading gradually through Spain and Italy to the North.

Evidence suggests that in early days the thread was held in the left hand and that the needles were hooked at one end like modern crochet hooks. Though implements of this type are, even now, not entirely obsolete, there is little doubt that by the Middle Ages straight pointed needles had come into general use. In this connection the 14th-century painting *The Visit of the Angels* (Plate 108), which once formed part of the altar of Buxtehude Abbey, is of particular interest. Here it will be seen that the Madonna is picking up the stitches round the neck of a garment, and that the needles and method of working are the same as those employed today. The fact that more than one thread is being used also indicates that at the time the picture was painted patterned knitting with different colours was an established practice in Europe.

In Britain, as in many other northern countries, it was among the wool-producing populations that knitting first developed into a highly skilled craft, and it is significant that the earliest references to knitting, which begin to appear about Edward IV's reign, concern warm and useful objects. In one such reference, from the *Records of the Borough of Nottingham*, it is stated that, in 1478, Isabel Capper obtained a licence to trade as a 'capknytter'. On the other hand, knitted stockings had not yet been seen here; hose consisted of pieces of cloth shaped and sewn together. John Skelton, poet laureate, describing the dress of a woman of the middle class at this period, wrote:

She hobbles as she goes
With her blanket hose,
Her shoon smeared with tallow.

70

The young King Edward VI is known to have received a formal present of a pair of knitted silk stockings from Sir Thomas Gresham, obtained, most probably, from Italy, where the itinerant stocking-maker was already a familiar figure. He may be seen in a drawing by Caracci (Fig. 7), plying his needles as he looks around for a possible customer. It will be noticed that he has, slung on his hip, a contrivance consisting of a board to which have been fixed two barrels, similar in principle to cotton barrels, and holding the two different threads with which he is working. Stow tells us that the first pair of worsted stockings to be knitted in this country were made in Queen Elizabeth

Fig. 7. *The Stocking Knitter*, by Annibale Caracci (1560–1609).

I's reign by William Rider, apprentice to Thomas Burdet, at the foot of London Bridge, who, having seen a pair at an Italian merchant's that had been brought from Mantua, copied them and presented them to the Earl of Pembroke.

In late medieval days knitting was still largely a masculine occupation. A man was required to serve an apprenticeship of six years before submitting his masterpiece to entitle him to full membership of his guild. A carpet by a master knitter might contain as many as twelve colours, while shirts and coats of silk and metal threads patterned with fruits and flowers, in purl and other raised stitches, rivalled those made from the richest brocades.

Although working with two or more straight pointed needles had for long been accepted in Western countries as the most efficient way of knitting, there was another method of producing a precisely similar fabric requiring tools of a very different kind. It was formerly known as peg- or ring-knitting, and survives today mainly among school-children, who may occasionally be seen knitting a cord with the aid of a reel, or a hollow cork, round the top of which a ring of tacks or pins has been set, from which it has acquired its modern name of 'corking'. The implement itself is known colloquially as a 'corking tube' or 'knitting nancy' (Plate 109).

To begin with, a knot is tied in the thread a short distance from the end, and is looped over one of the pegs, the loose end being pushed down through the centre of the cork. The first row of loops is made by twisting the thread once round each peg so that the loops point outwards, working in a clockwise direction. After this the thread is simply passed outside the pegs, and each loop, in turn, is lifted with a crochet hook or stiletto over it, and over the top of the peg. The cord, which protrudes through the hollow centre of the implement as it lengthens, is tubular, its thickness depending not only on the thread used but on the size, number and spacing of the pins or pegs.

For making piping cords, much used in the 16th and 17th centuries, a narrow tube of wood or ivory closely set round with fine pins was required; for a loosely knit, soft cord, three or four pegs at wider intervals sufficed. The large ivory implement in Plate 110, its handle carefully turned to fit the grasp of the fingers, was probably once used in a monastery for making the girdles worn by the monks. Ring-knitting was also employed in earlier centuries for making caps, bags, pockets and scarves. In this case fifty or more pegs might be needed, mounted in a circle (centre Plate 109) or on a strip of board with the two rows of pegs facing one another across a central slit.

A much more primitive device, employed by the North American Indians, for knitting a flat girdle, is illustrated on the right of Plate 109. Here a number of short sticks are placed side by side so that they may be held in the hand. The method is, again, that of peg-knitting, though the thread in this instance is manipulated entirely with the fingers.

The year 1589 must be regarded as a landmark in the history of knitting, for it was in that year that William Lee, a native of Calverton or Woodborough in Nottinghamshire, and a scholar of St John's College, Cambridge, invented the stocking frame. This was an ingenious device, the forerunner of the modern knitting machine, on which he made not only stockings but waistcoats and other garments, thus arousing the bitter opposition of the hand knitters, who feared that their livelihood might be threatened. Lee applied to Queen Elizabeth for protection and encouragement, but his petition was refused. Unable to find any support for his invention in England, he settled in France, taking many of his work-people with him. Here again he met with frustration, and he is said to have died of a broken heart in Paris, in 1610. The acceptance of his machine was nevertheless only a matter of time. Evelyn, in his Diary, on May 3rd, 1661, wrote: 'I went to see the wonderfull engine for weaving silk stockings, said to have ben the invention of an Oxford (*sic*) Scholler 40 years since.'

Two years later the Company of Frame-work knitters received their Charter from Charles II. A painting of William Lee, pointing to one of his iron frames and discoursing to a woman knitting with needles and her fingers, was formerly in the possession of the Company. Beneath it was the following quaint inscription: 'In the year 1589, the ingenious William Lee, A.M. of St John's College, Cambridge, devised this profitable art for stockings, (but being despised went to France,) yet of iron to himself, but to us and to others of gold, in memory of whom this is here painted.' This picture has unfortunately been lost since about 1773; a Victorian painting of the same subject is now in Nottingham Castle.

The new invention had little effect on the domestic knitting that was practised of necessity in most households, often as an alternative to weaving. Many a family had its own long strip or sampler of patterns, carefully preserved from one generation to another. The distinctive Fair Isle patterns of the Shetland knitters are said to date back to the days when Spanish sailors, shipwrecked from the Armada, sought refuge on the Island and taught the inhabitants this elaborate method of working. Occasionally designs were made out in the form of charts with symbols to indicate the various stitches. Written directions are a comparatively modern introduction; they would, indeed, have been of little use in an age when few people could read.

In the Yorkshire Dales children were taught to knit as soon as they were old enough to hold their needles. Sitting in groups they chanted the traditional knitting songs, handed down through many centuries, in which the words and rhythm of each verse bore some reference to the round being knitted and the number of stitches to be increased or decreased. Both men and women gossiped over their knitting as they jogged their way to market; shepherds knitted as they guarded their flocks. Celia Fiennes, in an account of her journey through East Anglia in 1698, speaks of the country lanes 'where you mete the ordinary people knitting 4 or 5 in a company under the hedges.'

As most households were dependent on the clothing they could themselves produce, rapidity in these days was of primary importance, and it was this necessity for speed that brought into use the knitting sheath, an implement worn on the right hip, tucked into the belt or apron string. Its purpose was to support the needle usually held in the right hand. At the top end of the sheath a hole was bored, approximately an inch in depth, and in this the needle was inserted. The fingers of the right hand now being completely free, could be held immediately over the points of the needles where they took over and manipulated the working thread much more rapidly than was possible with the older method; in some instances long, curved needles known as pricks were used, bringing the work nearer to the eyes of the knitter.

Most knitting sheaths in this country were fashioned from wood, and are from five to twelve inches in length. As they were frequently made and given as love tokens they often bear a date and the initials of the donor and recipient. There are a few known examples with late 17th-century dates, but the majority belong to the 18th and early 19th centuries. Early knitting sheaths are usually rectangular in section, tapering towards the base; the example dated 1709 in Plate 111 is typical of this period, with delicate chip-carving and a diagonal groove on one side to secure it to the apron string. In some cases the groove is V-shaped, or the sheath may be carved with a prong or deep slot at the back to enable it to fit over a waistband.

Many of these early sheaths, or sticks as they are sometimes called, were made by sailors, or rural swains, anxious to exhibit their skill in carving. Hollowed out window or lantern-and-ball decoration is often found in conjunction with chip-carving, and hearts entwined with amorous sentiments or mottoes may also appear. Spindle-shaped knitting sticks, lathe-turned or carved by hand, were used in the wool-growing districts of the north-west, and may be equally old but are seldom dated; the apron string in this case rested in one of the grooves, or was twisted round the neck of the sheath.

Very different in type is the scimitar or goose-wing sheath (fourth from the left in Plate 111). Here the short shaft which holds the needle is set in a broad blade shaped to fit over the curve of the hip. The engraved metal band at the top of the haft has on it, in rolled or knurled lettering, the words 'For auld lang syne', from which it might be inferred that the sheath came from Scotland. In fact, this is unlikely, as this type of implement is peculiar to the Lake District and the surrounding counties; the band, in this instance, has been made from the base of a silver thimble probably of Scottish origin.

Of inscriptions, other than an initial or date, amorous or sentimental phrases are the most usual, though even these are by no means common; religious texts are very occasionally found. The sheath on the extreme right of Plate 112 is carved with the head of Nelson and 'England expects every man this day will do his duty'. It will be noted that some sheaths are carved at the lower end in the form of a chain terminating in a hook or barb. If fashioned all in one piece this was, of course, additional evidence of the carver's skill, but the device also served a very definite purpose. When the implement was in position the chain was taken round at the back of the wearer and the hook inserted in the work, as soon as it became long enough, to support it and give the right 'pull'.

The position of the hook was changed as the work grew, for, to an expert knitter, tension was of great importance. In some instances the chain has a central swivel to allow a greater freedom of movement. Yorkshire knitters used a metal hook, known as 'the top crook', for this same purpose; it was either attached to the belt or tied on to a piece of tape that could be wound round the waist and tightened as required.

By the end of the 18th century the delicate carving of earlier years had virtually disappeared, though the knitting sticks themselves became more varied. Birds, fishes and grotesque figures are among the more familiar forms to be found at this period. Heart-shaped sheaths had also come into use; these might be of wood, metal or stiffened embroidery, with a short shaft attached, and were either sewn or pinned on to the clothing above the right hip. Other, more simply contrived devices, that took the place of a knitting stick, were a straw-filled cushion, a bunch of quills, or a leather pouch, all of which could be attached to the waistbelt and into which a needle could be thrust.

While in these islands wool knitting remained predominantly a peasant craft, in other countries it was more widely diffused, particularly in Germany and Austria where it was considered as elegant an occupation as knotting or netting. In consequence foreign knitting sheaths are often more elaborate or made of more costly materials. The four straight spindle-shaped sheaths in Plate 114 come from the Continent, and are of silver with a ring attached through which a ribbon or cord could be threaded. In the centre of the same illustration is a rare porcelain knitting stick, perhaps from Spain, with gilt and multi-coloured decoration, slightly curved to fit over the hip. Other foreign examples are made of ivory, amber, shagreen, or maybe of wood or metal covered with twisted silks and straw veneer.

A remarkable collection of carved boxwood sheaths from the Pinto Collection may be seen in Plate 113. The two on the extreme left are Italian; the third German or Flemish; the fourth is Dutch, the main motif of the carving being Faith, Hope, Charity and Justice; the fifth, carved with a lizard, is Italian and silver mounted; while the sixth, Swiss or Tyrolean, has on it two figures, a violinist and a flautist. Below is a superbly made French knitting sheath with masterly, small-scale, precision repetition carving.

To prevent the stitches from slipping off the needles when the work was laid aside expanding protectors made of silver were used, with hollow tips that fitted over the needles; in Germany and Austria these were sometimes worn suspended from the waist by an ornamental chain or clasp. A more usual object in this country, serving the same purpose, was a narrow, cylindrical case of wood or ivory, about ten inches in length, unscrewing at one end and with a long, central slit through which the knitting could protrude (Plate 111). This was later superseded by a device consisting of a pair of short, conical tips of ivory or wood joined by a length of elastic, a method of protection that has persisted to the present day (Plate 115).

In early Georgian times patterned knitting in coloured silks was a fashionable occupation among people with leisure. Many sets of fine steel needles were therefore made, and may be found today in old bodkin or netting-needle cases. They were used mainly for making small bags, purses and pincushions, and, by men, for knitting garters. Another, very decorative, form of work for which fine needles were required was bead-knitting. This is not the same as beaded knitting where steel or other beads, strung on the working thread, are moved up at intervals to lie between the stitches. In bead-knitting a single bead is pushed through the loop of every stitch; the front surface of the work is thus entirely composed of beads and, if joins are to be avoided, the complete pattern must be threaded row by row before knitting commences.

A remarkable example of multi-coloured bead-knitting of the 18th century may be seen in Plate 117. It is seamless, having been made on three or more needles to fit the outside of a round, leather-covered box; some idea of the fineness of the work may be obtained from the fact that it is knitted at a tension of no fewer than twenty-six stitches or beads to the inch so that, in all, approximately 25,000 beads must have been used.

By the end of George II's reign yet another era was dawning in the history of knitting. The new light-coloured prints and muslins that were being imported in increasing quantities from the East had brought with them a fashion for white stockings, socks and gloves, made from fine cotton yarns. As the century progressed, white knitting became more and more popular, for, whereas silk knitting had been only for the few, cotton was within the reach of nearly everyone's purse. The heavy duty imposed on foreign laces had, moreover, encouraged the use of trimmings knitted in fine white thread. Patterns grew increasingly intricate and stitches still smaller; collars and cuffs, mittens, fichus, bonnets and doyleys, in delicate lace-like designs were made throughout the Georgian period (Plate 118).

For this work special needles were manufactured of so fine a gauge that they were little thicker than ordinary sewing needles; many of them were 'blued' in the centre to show up the white stitches. The vogue for white knitting also brought with it what is sometimes described as a peculiar fashion for wearing gloves while working; but this was more than a fashion—it was a wise precaution to prevent the moisture from the hands staining the white thread.

Meanwhile, throughout the 18th century, the more homely craft of wool knitting continued to flourish. In villages and country towns old people sat at their doors on summer evenings, their needles moving briskly backwards and forwards; at their feet stood a wicker cage imprisoning a ball of wool, or, perhaps, a smoothly turned wooden wool-bowl so shaped that the ball, when placed in it, would revolve without escaping as the yarn was drawn out (Plate 45). Here and there, on their way to market, a man or woman could be seen with a small netted bag hanging from the waistbelt in which a ball of wool was entrapped, for people still knitted as they jogged their way through the country lanes. Lady Eleanor Butler, one of the 'Ladies of Llangollen', describing a Fair at Llangollen in 1781, wrote: 'What a picture might be drawn from our parlour window of the crowds descending the opposite mountain . . . the women knitting as they went along.'

In spite of the increasing use of machinery and the development of the factory system at the beginning of the 19th century, as a result of which ready-made clothing became obtainable at the shops, those with large families to support found home knitting as essential as ever. The elaborately decorated sheaths of earlier generations had passed out of favour, but in mid-Victorian times women in the Black Country might be seen with a piece of felt, with a hole in it, pinned to their skirts, in which a knitting needle was lodged. Even half a century later, among the poorest members of the community, speed in knitting was still of importance. That painstaking student of social history, M. K. Ashby, has recorded that, in her childhood in the late 1880s, in the village of Tysoe in Warwickshire, a woman with a knitting-pin holder twisted into the waist-tapes of her linen apron was no uncommon sight.

9

Netting, Net-work and Needle-made Lace

THE ORIGINS of netting lie so far back in time that it is impossible to trace its early history. Its uses, moreover, are so varied and so widespread that it cannot be associated with any particular country or clime. The fisherman, the sailor, the fowler and the hunter all required nets for their different occupations; the farmer used them for many purposes on the land, and the housewife needed them for penning in her poultry, storing her vegetables for winter use and protecting the fruit trees in her garden from the ravages of birds.

The tools used were, at first, extremely simple. For a shuttle, all that was required was a strip of wood having a V-shaped cut at either end, and sufficiently thin to pass through the mesh when wound with thread; another short piece of wood formed the gauge. Later, for making smaller meshes, a netting-needle was sometimes used; this was similar to the shuttle though much finer, and was fashioned from iron, steel or bone, with an open loop at either end. Implements of this type were in use in Roman Britain, and differed little from those employed today (Plate 119).

The use of netting for decorative purposes was probably introduced into Europe from the Orient by returning crusaders in the 11th and 12th centuries; veils of gold and silver mesh had, from very early times, formed part of the traditionally gorgeous raiment of the East. The embroidery of net in geometrical patterns with coloured silks was known in the West, during the 13th and 14th centuries, as *opus areneum*: in English, Spiderwork. The use of fine white netting as a form of lace for edgings and insertions was a later development. It was closely connected with the introduction of white embroidery which, during the 15th century, was coming gradually into fashion, principally for the ornamentation of the linen underclothing that had supplanted the heavy and often unwashable garments of earlier years.

When embroidering linen, it was found that a lighter effect could be obtained if some of the warp and woof threads were drawn out of the material and the remaining loosened threads were buttonholed over or clustered together with a looped stitch. Rectangular pieces could also be cut away, the raw edges being oversewn, while long stitches taken from corner to corner formed diagonal bars on which elaborate patterns could be built up. Eventually so much of the area to be decorated was cut or drawn away that little remained except a network of threads or buttonholed bars serving as a background for further embroidery.

It was in this manner that the needle-made lace that we now know as reticella work developed, the name being derived from the Italian *rete*, a net (Plate 133). At the same time it became apparent that an extremely delicate effect could be obtained if, instead of withdrawing the threads from linen, a background of netted mesh was used. As in the East, therefore, delicate netting tools were fashioned, and strips and panels of fine-gauge mesh were made from linen thread and stretched in a light wire frame to be embroidered and inserted in, or added to, the material as and when required.

During the 16th century the vogue for white net-work spread rapidly across Europe, from the Mediterranean countries to England and farther north, the character of the work varying according to the country of its adoption. In France, for instance, where it was known as *filet* or *lacis*, the pattern was formed by filling in the squares of the mesh with two darning stitches: *point de reprise*, in which needle and thread are taken in and out of the mesh in one direction only, and *point de toile*, or cloth stitch, in which the threads are interwoven in both directions. As a rule no other stitches were used (Plate 134), a fact which gave the work a dignity and simplicity of its own.

One of the main advantages of *filet* lace was that the regularity of the mesh made it possible to reproduce with ease any designs or lettering set out on squared paper. In England it became known as holy lace, as it was much used for ecclesiastical embroidery; religious symbols, texts and Biblical pictures were darned on strips of white netting and inserted into linen vestments and altar frontals. At the beginning of the 17th century there was a singular fashion for ornamenting household linen and underclothing in the same manner, as may be seen from the following description of a needlewoman in Jasper Mayne's *The City Match*:

> *She works religious petticoats, for flowers*
> *She'll make church histories, her needle doth*
> *So sanctify my cushionets, besides*
> *My smock sleeves have such holy embroideries*
> *And are so learned, that I fear in time*
> *All my apparel will be quoted by*
> *Some pious instructor.*

This verse was written in 1630, and the same fashion is referred to in *The Custom of the Country*, a play written in 1628, in which a character remarks: 'Sure you should not be without a neat historical shirt.'

In Germany and Scandinavia the technique of net embroidery was much more elaborate, a shaded effect being obtained by the use of an innumerable variety of stitches and threads of different thicknesses (Plate 126), while in Italy an even more decorative effect was obtained by the combination of embroidery with the skilful use of different size gauges in forming the mesh.

In this country the vogue for white net-work was followed by a fashion for coloured silk netting which was used for a wide variety of purposes and continued throughout the 18th century. During George I's reign Mary Blackstone and William Hay, at the sign of the Blue Boar in Cheapside, were advertising 'all sorts of silk twist for the making of purses and of partridge nets'.[1] An account of a wedding in 1786, in Mrs Delany's memoirs, contains a description of the clothes worn by both bride and bridegroom, the latter, it is stated, wearing a very pretty waistcoat 'that she net him'.

For all these different types of work sets of carefully graded tools were needed. Those of ivory or tortoiseshell were often contained in cylindrical cases fashioned from the same material (Plate 120). Netting-needle cases of Eastern origin might be covered with galuchat, or made from metal, enamelled or ornamented with gold or silver wire. Others, from France and Italy, were decorated with straw marquetry (Plate 121). In addition to the shuttles and gauges a bodkin-like implement was provided for use when only a short length of thread was available, and in some netting-needle cases there was also a small flat hook for joining and finishing edges. If beading was introduced, the shuttle was replaced by an ordinary fine sewing needle with which the beads could be picked up and moved along the thread as required.

It is essential when netting that the foundation loop, into which the first row of the mesh is worked, should be attached to some firm object against which it may be held taut. With coarse work this loop, known as the stirrup, and made of tape or string, was placed underneath the foot; but for fine netting such a method of working was obviously impractical. Lead-weighted cushions were therefore made that could be placed on a table, the loop being secured by means of a pin (Plate 79). A later development was the wooden or ivory knob that may sometimes be seen on 18th- and 19th-century sewing and winding clamps over which a netting loop could be slipped, while small cut-steel clamps, intended solely for netting, were surmounted by a solitary knob or hook (see Chapter 6).

[1] From *The Russells in Bloomsbury 1669-1771*, by Gladys Scott Thomson. Cape, 1940.

A much more elaborate device, which came into use in the latter half of the 18th century, was the netting-box, rectangular in shape, about nine inches long and five inches wide and containing not only shuttles and gauges but a small roller with a slit or holes to which a foundation loop could be attached. The roller was provided with a handle and ratchet so that the work could be wound up to a convenient length as it increased. The fashionably dressed lady on the extreme right of the engraving illustrated in Plate 123, who is making a narrow strip of netting, has a device of this kind on her knee. A more detailed illustration of a French netting-box, made in the form of a book, may be seen in Plates 121 and 122. Here the roller is hinged to the side of the box and, when the lid is open, can be raised and secured in an upright position by a metal pin. The whole box is decorated inside and out with straw-work, even the roller and its handle being carefully veneered with straw in shades of rose, green and gold.

It was evidently a device of this kind that Betsy Sheridan, sister of the playwright, bought at a toyshop in Tunbridge Wells in 1785, as a present for her sister Alicia, for in a letter accompanying the parcel she says: 'There is a box for you to put your netting in while you work it, and to keep it in when you are idle, with lock and key.' Some of the larger work-boxes of the late 18th and early 19th centuries have special compartments fitted with roller and ratchet that served a similar purpose. They were used mainly for netting purses.

It is by no means unusual, in an old work-box, to find large wooden shuttles and gauges side by side with more delicate implements of ivory, tortoiseshell and steel, for with the progress of the centuries coarse netting for purely practical purposes had lost none of its importance, and a skilled needle-woman did not hesitate to include such work among her activities. Mrs Delany, on a visit to Bulstrode in 1783, found the Duchess of Portland occupied in making a cherry net of 100 meshes per row.

Instructions for domestic netting dating from this same period include directions for making a fowling or gaming net of packthread, to be dyed brown by steeping it in a tanner's pit, or a light green by boiling it in water with young wheat shoots, or a yellow by soaking it in a decoction of celandine. The first was intended for use on ploughed fields, the second on grass and the third on stubble lands. Netting was one of the few drawing-room occupations permitted to men; Augustus Hare records that, as a boy, he was allowed no other indoor pastime. Parson Kilvert, in his diary, mentions that in the winter of 1870 he was employed in 'making a net for the morella cherry tree against the north wall of the house'.

For many people, nevertheless, netting was much more than a pastime:

Her Father he makes cabbage-nets
And through the streets does cry 'em,

wrote Henry Carey at the beginning of the 18th century in *Sally in our Alley*. In coastal areas, where the needs of fishermen ensured a constant demand, net-making was an important home industry, shuttles and gauges of varying sizes were to be found in every cottage, while a box of tools for mending nets was, and still is, a necessary part of a sailor's equipment.

With the development of the factory system at the end of the 18th century continual efforts were made to devise some means of making net by mechanical methods, but it was not until comparatively recent times that a machine was invented that could make a knot in a length of string.

Meanwhile, at the beginning of the 19th century, the stocking-frame workers and the Nottingham lace-makers, occupied with the same problem, had succeeded in producing a machine-made mesh of looped or twisted threads which, though of little use where strength was required, served many other practical purposes. In needlework it could be employed most effectively, being much finer than anything that could be made by hand. The embroidress, therefore, laid aside her shuttles and gauges and, using this new, gossamer-like material as a background, found fresh opportunities for her skill in the finest and most delicate stitchery. Examples of late Georgian net-work may be seen in Plates 125 and 129, and may be contrasted with the older net embroidery in Plate 126.

This history of hand-netting was not, however, at an end. During the mid Victorian era it enjoyed a period of popularity as a pastime for young ladies. Searching out the fine shuttles and gauges that had been discarded by their mothers and grandmothers, they made doyleys, shawls and antimacassars, of cotton, wool and silk, sometimes ornamented with simple darning stitches (Plate 127). As, however, the Nottingham lace-makers were now not only producing fine net, but reproducing all kinds of lace cheaply and effectively with the aid of the Jacquard Loom, the revival was only brief, and fine netting and net-work, though they by no means disappeared, went gradually out of fashion.

In tracing the history of net-work mention was made at the beginning of this chapter of the introduction of white openwork embroidery in the latter half of the 15th century. This work was later brought to perfection in Italy; it consisted of drawn-work (*punto tirato*) in which a number of threads were withdrawn from the material, and cut-work (*punto tagliato*) in which portions of the fabric itself were cut away. In drawn-work the pattern was formed by clustering together the loosened warp and woof threads or whipping them over with buttonhole stitches. In cut-work the raw edges of the rectangular spaces were sewn over, while long stitches, taken from corner to corner, were formed into buttonholed bars serving as a support for more extensive embroidery.

This led to the development of the geometrical reticella laces and eventually to the other more free and elaborate needle-made laces of the 17th century, for it was found that patterns could be built up quite independently of the material by using a strip of parchment on which the outlines of the design were drawn. The parchment was placed over two layers of linen, to which it was attached round the edge with stitching, and was sometimes supported by a cushion or circular basket (Fig. 8). Several threads were then laid along the

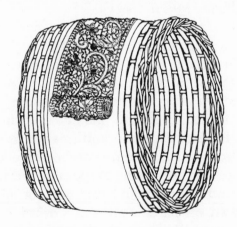

Fig. 8. Lace-maker's basket, for use in needlepoint. Light and easily turned in all directions, it rested on the worker's knees, supporting the lace and raising it near to the eyes.

outlines of the design and fixed to the parchment and the underlying linen by means of tacking stitches, thus forming a skeleton or framework upon which the lace could be constructed.

The main portions of the design were filled in with closely worked buttonhole stitches and joined together by buttonholed bars or *brides*, the surrounding mesh being composed of tiny looped stitches. Finally, when the work was completed, a knife was drawn between the two layers of linen, cutting the tacking threads and releasing the lace from the parchment. As the lace had been built up stitch upon stitch and not in association with a material as in drawn and cut work, it was named, very aptly, *punto in aria*: literally 'stitch in air'.

It was from such simple beginnings that the intricate needlepoint or parchment laces of Italy eventually evolved, proving formidable rivals to the pillow laces of France, the Netherlands and this country. The two kinds of work are, nevertheless, quite distinct. Needlepoint lace is derived from surface embroidery, no other tools than the needle and thread being required. Pillow lace has its origins in the plaiting of braids or 'laces', as they were originally termed, the numerous threads of metal, silk or linen being wound on to specially made bobbins (see Chapter 14).

There is, however, one type of needle-made lace that has much in common with drawn and cut work, for which a special device was evolved, namely Teneriffe-work or Sun Lace. This had its origin in a form of needlework called *Sols* that was cultivated in Spain during the 16th century, in which circular holes of varying sizes were cut in material, the spaces being filled in with embroidery on radiating threads. The work soon spread to Southern and Central America and to the Canary Islands, where it was further developed, the embroidered circles now being made independently and attached to, or inserted in, the material afterwards (Plates 130 and 131).

Originally, for this type of lace, the circle with the required number of radiants was first drawn on parchment. The circumference was then pricked round at regular intervals at the points were it was met by the radiants, and a single line of running stitches was worked in and out of these holes. A long length of thread was next wound on to a fine netting needle and taken backwards and forwards across the circle, through opposite pairs of the running stitches, until sufficient radiants were formed. A second and smaller circle of running stitches was sometimes made from which a number of shorter radiants could be stretched to the circumference, thus preventing too great an accumulation of threads in the centre. Elaborate borders and insertions of joining and intersecting circles could be drawn on parchment and worked in the same way; when the embroidery was finished the tacking stitches were cut, and the lace released.

Eventually the process was much simplified by the adoption of a lace tablet, consisting of a disc of bone or ivory notched round the edge or, alternatively, two circular pieces of cardboard cemented together, covered with waxed cloth or paper, and stuck round with glass-headed pins (Plate 128). The use of a netting needle was no longer necessary, as the thread could now be wound direct from the skein or ball onto the tablet round the notches, or the heads of the pins. It will be noted that, in the large tablet illustrated, the centre has been left hollow, the lace in this instance being intended as a trimming for a doyley. Teneriffe work was extremely popular in England in the Victorian era, but went out of fashion at the beginning of this century. In Italy, and other countries where it is still made, squares, oblongs and triangles are variants of the older and more familiar circles.

Knotting and Tatting

THE PRACTICE of knotting thread or cord for use in embroidery was well known in this country in late medieval times, but did not become at all general until the end of the 17th century. The thread required was first wound on a shuttle, and by means of this a series of picots or knots was made in it at close intervals, so that it formed a narrow trimming bearing some resemblance to a string of beads. Afterwards it was couched down in patterns on to linen or other materials with fine stitching. A remarkable example of this type of work may be seen illustrated in Plate 139. This doublet, dating from about 1630, is thought to have belonged to John Carter, a leading Parliamentarian during the Civil War, and Bailiff of Yarmouth in the years 1641 and 1651. It is of linen, partially lined with gold satin; the knotted linen threads couched on to the fabric are interspersed with French knots also in linen thread.

It was probably the Dutch, through their close contacts with the English Court in the 17th century, who popularised this method of working in England, for Holland at this time had extensive trading relations with the East, and the Chinese made frequent and skilful use of knotted lines in their embroideries. Knotting was a pleasant occupation, requiring little concentration, that could be taken up at times when closer work would have been impossible, as after continual repetition the movements of the shuttle became almost mechanical. It was a pastime much favoured at Court in the reign of William and Mary. The Queen herself was an ardent knotter as we know from Sir Charles Sedley's often quoted lines:

> *For here's a Queen now thanks to God!*
> *Who when she rides in coach abroad*
> *Is always knotting threads.*

One of the best-known examples of knotted-line embroidery existing today is a large hanging of linen worked by Princess Amelia, daughter of George II. It is fringed on three sides, and ornamented with knotting in linen thread.

85

Mrs Delany who, throughout her long life, makes constant mention in her letters of the knotting she is engaged upon, wrote to her sister in 1750: 'I have no knotting of the sort you want done. I cannot promise too much for you until I have finished a plain fringe I am knotting to trim a new blue and white linen bed I have just put up; as soon as that is finished I will do some sugar-plum for you . . . send me the sized knotting you want. I have a good knotting friend that I can employ, I believe, for you.' The 'sugar-plum' referred to consisted of large raised knots or picots used for appliqué in the more elaborate parts of the embroidery.

The shuttles used for this type of work were generally one to two inches in width and about four to six inches long; the exact dimensions were unimportant as the size of the knotting did not depend on the implement but on the thickness of the thread employed. In old shuttles, it will be noted, there is a considerable space between the tips of the blades (Plate 140); this was to enable them to be wound with silk cords or coarse homespun yarns with which the heavy counterpanes and bed-hangings of former times were sometimes decorated.

As might be expected of implements designed for use in royal circles, they were exquisitely made, often of the most costly materials. Those of ivory and tortoiseshell are the most numerous, the latter occasionally ornamented with inlay of pearl, silver or different coloured golds (Plate 136). Equally elaborate are the shuttles fashioned from finely pierced and cut steel (Plates 137 and 138), or of silver with filigree decoration; other materials used were rock crystal, amber, porcelain, vernis Martin, Chinese lacquer, horn, and woods of various kinds which might be painted (Plate 141), or veneered with straw. Mrs Delany, in 1763, referred to 'a very elegant shuttle' bought for two guineas, and again, in 1783, to 'a gold knotting shuttle of most exquisite workmanship and taste' that George III had just presented to her.

French knotting shuttles were often much larger than those used in this country and were the most ornate. Their practical use was of secondary importance, as they were employed very largely for effect. A woman in fashionable society learned to wield her shuttle as she would her fan. Each implement fitted into its own small *sac*, elaborately embroidered, and was taken from place to place in an extravagantly large and beribboned knotting-bag which was carried to routs, assemblies and theatrical performances. Madame de Genlis, in her *Dictionary of Court Ceremonial*, maintained that knotting had no other purpose than to enable a woman to appear composed when in company. The shuttle or *navette*, she states, is an emblem: 'a symbol, expressing the aversion which all females ought to have to complete idleness', at the same time allowing them to take up attitudes that characterise feminine grace. It is for this reason that the work was called *Frivolité*, the name by which its successor, Tatting, is still known today.

In France knotting shuttles were frequently given as presents. The following charming quatrain accompanied a gold shuttle that the Duchesse de Villeroi gave to Madame la Comtesse de Brionne:

> *L'emblème frappe ici vos yeux.*
> *Si les graces, l'amour et l'amitié parfaite*
> *Peuvent jamais former des noeuds,*
> *Vous devez tenir la navette.*

It is recorded that, in 1745, the Infanta Maria Theresa found among her wedding presents five caskets of enamelled gold, each with its shuttle, valued at more than 4000 livres. The Day Book of Lazare Duvaux contains several references to shuttles bought for the great courtesan Madame de Pompadour, the most elaborate of gold, with enamelled branches hung with cherries formed of cornelian stones and costing 550 livres. There is also mention of a shuttle bought for a child for 192 livres, an indication that, in royal circles, instruction in the art of graceful movement began at an early age. Horace Walpole, however, in an account of his presentation at the French Court in 1765, refers, somewhat ungallantly, to the daughters of Louis XV as 'the four Mesdames who are clumsy, plump old wenches, with black cloaks and knotting-bags'. In this same year Walpole himself bought three knotting-bags in Paris, at the request of his friend Lady Hervey, and arranged for them to be smuggled into this country.

Posters and newspaper advertisements sometimes contained announcements regarding knotting shuttles which their owners had lost and were anxious to recover. On May 11th, 1767, the Comtesse de Ranes, living in the Rue de l'Enfer, Paris, offered a reward to any person returning to her a shuttle of pierced gold, of which the middle represented the attributes of Cupid in various coloured golds. Another advertisement stated that 'there was lost at the Comédie Française, or on leaving the performance, a bag of silk in which was a shuttle of shell mounted in gold'. The same newspaper also announced the loss of 'a gold coloured shuttle, filled with gold covered silk thread, in a bag of rose coloured taffeta embroidered with silver'.

Knotting needles are often referred to at this period. In 1762, Henrietta Hotham, who was then nine years old and was staying at Marble Hill with her great-aunt Lady Suffolk, wrote home to her mother for 'a small knotting needle, round at both Ends, and a pound of the best Thread for mine and my aunt's use'. Though a shuttle is, of course, a form of needle, as it conveys the working thread, what was meant here was probably a netting-needle which was sometimes used in fine knotting. Alternatively, Lady Suffolk may have been teaching her great-niece to net: netting was occasionally referred to as knotting, to which it is so closely allied.

While in England, and on the Continent, few women cared to sit for their portraits when occupied with more ordinary forms of needlework, to be painted while knotting was considered particularly elegant. The work itself was, of course, of little significance, the shuttle and thread serving merely to secure a graceful poise. Towards the end of the 18th century, however, the fashion for knotting declined. The embroidered and beribboned bags were used for other kinds of work, and the large shuttles, once laid aside, began to find their way into the hands of collectors. At the sale of the Duc de Lorraine's possessions, which took place in Brussels in September, 1781, no less than seventeen knotting shuttles were listed, some of them of the very finest craftsmanship. In this country, in the Wallace Collection, there are two French knotting shuttles representative of the period (Plate 138).

The transition from knotting to tatting, as we now understand the term, was a gradual one. The object of the former was to provide a decorative line or cord for appliqué in surface embroidery. Tatting, on the other hand, although involving a similar technique, was used for creating patterns and trimmings entire in themselves, usually in white thread and serving the same purpose as lace. The shuttles were small and pointed at the ends (Plate 143). In Italy, where it is said to have originated in the 16th century, the work was known as *occhi* from the 'eyes' or rings of which it is composed. These rings were made in rows and clusters which were joined afterwards by tying or stitching; for this reason, it is said, the work acquired its English name of tatting, being made up of many bits and pieces. At a later stage trimmings, mats and counterpanes were made by combining tatting with crochet. The silver-gilt donkeys in Plate 164 carry a shuttle and six graded hooks in their panniers.

Eventually, with the development of new techniques involving the use of fine netting-needles and even sewing needles, it was found possible to join the motifs while working the pattern, thus dispensing with the tedious processes of tying or stitching. At the same time the introduction of small purls or picots, made at intervals on the outside edge of the rings, gave the tatting a lighter and more delicate appearance (Plate 148). A still further advance was the introduction of a second shuttle; the Victorian tatting-box in Plate 145, it will be noticed, contains a pair of shuttles with blades meeting closely at the tip to prevent the thread unwinding too readily, a necessary precaution with this method of working. In addition, the box contains a large pin, known as a purling-pin, to serve as a gauge over which the picots could be formed.

For more elaborate patterns in which picots of varying lengths were introduced, sets of purling-pins or gauges of varying sizes could be obtained. A pin or hook was also needed for pulling through the connecting loops as the work progressed. This last process was further simplified by the use of a tatting-ring to which a small hook was attached by a short metal chain; the ring was worn on the left thumb while working, the hook being picked up easily with the right hand whenever required. The elegant gold tatting tool, in the form of a hairpin, illustrated in Plate 143, served the same purpose though, in this instance, the chain to which it is attached was fasteneed in some convenient position to the dress.

Two other more uncommon tools, devised to simplify the work, are a shuttle with closed ends having a small flat reel between the blades on to which the thread is wound by inserting a key into a square hole on one side; another is shaped like the egg capsule of the skate, with one of the two curved 'claws' at either end elongated, thus combining shuttle and hook in one. The latter tool is an invention of comparatively modern times, for the search for new forms and new methods still continues.

With regard to the evolution of tatting in this country, there can be little doubt that it owes much of its development to the efforts of those two indefatigable needlewomen Mlle Eleanore Riego and Mlle Thérèse de Dillmont, who did so much in the latter part of the last century to establish and popularise many little-known forms of needlework. Though Mlle Riego's claim to have introduced tatting into England cannot now be substantiated, with the restricted communications and limited knowledge of her times she may well have thought her methods of working to be a complete innovation.

In this respect, the Diary of Parson Woodforde once again provides information that is of particular interest. In March, 1781, he writes: 'To two ivory shuttles for Nancy, of Baker, paid 0.1.0.' Again, in May of the following year, he buys 'a fine tortoiseshell shuttle' for his niece. This latter implement was probably for knotting, still a fashionable pastime in this country; but the ivory shuttles, at sixpence apiece, can only have been small and were, most probably, a pair. As Parson Woodforde is always detailed in the description he gives of the sewing implements he frequently purchased, it may reasonably be assumed that in 1781, in a remote village in Norfolk, Nancy Woodforde was already tatting, possibly with two shuttles.

Embroidery and Cord-making

THE TYPE of needlework for which this country was most celebrated in the early middle ages was an elaborate form of surface embroidery, employed mainly for the decoration of church vestments, and involving the extensive use of metal thread. By the 13th century English ecclesiastical embroidery was unrivalled in Europe; the work had, in fact, become known as *Opus Anglicanum*. In the unsettled conditions of the next two centuries the demand for this form of needlework declined, and in consequence the style of the work itself became impoverished.

With the period of comparative peace and prosperity, ushered in by the reign of Henry VII, however, a new era was dawning. The fashion for luxurious living set by Henry VIII and his Court brought about a renewed demand for elaborate embroidery, particularly for heraldic and costume embroidery, and it is significant that when, in 1561, the Broderers Company was revived and received its Charter from Elizabeth I, it was the tools of the gold-worker that appeared on the arms. In the centre of a fesse (Fig. 9) are two broches crossing one another and on either side a spool or quill wound with gold thread: in heraldic terms *'on a fesse gules two broches in saltire between as many quills or'*.

The broche, or spindle, is a wooden implement about eight inches long used by the embroiderer for laying the gold and not, as is so often stated, a piercing tool. The handle, by which it is manipulated, has a triangular base to keep it from rolling when laid on a table. The metal thread is wound on to the bobbin in the centre of the implement, over a padding of cotton-wool, and the end passed through the deep cleft at the point. Once this loose end has been attached to the work the thread can be unwound and laid in position without coming into contact with the hands, a matter of primary importance where gold and silver are concerned.

At the top of Fig. 9 is a mellore, a steel tool of very ancient origin, about four inches long, also of much value to the gold worker in helping to place or flatten an unruly thread, the sharp point serving as a piercer for making holes in the material through which coarse threads could be passed if required. The term mellore may be a corruption of *mettre l'or*, or, possibly, of *menne-lourd* (*mener l'or*), the name formerly applied to a modelling tool of box-wood or ivory that was used for leading the gold thread over the moulded surfaces in heavily raised work.

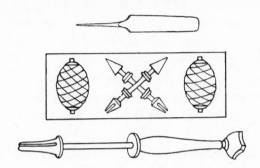

Fig. 9. (*above*) Steel mellore for use in gold work and (*below*) wooden broche for laying gold thread. (*centre*) Two broches with a quill of gold thread on either side, from the Arms of the Broderers' Company

The frame, or tent, used by a professional embroiderer was composed of two long and two short pieces of wood, with a series of holes in each, and fixed together at the four corners by means of pegs; it was thus readily adjustable, ensuring an even pull on the material in both directions. It was extremely large, but light enough to be lifted easily on and off the supporting trestles. In the engraving of an 18th-century embroiderers' workshop in Plate 149 the woman on the left is holding up a frame of this type which, as may be seen, holds a sufficient length of material for making a complete front of a man's coat or waistcoat. The flap of a pocket will also be seen outlined upon the fabric. Cuffs, collars, borders and buttons were all prepared and worked in the frame, to be cut round afterwards and made up by the tailor.

Such embroidery was, of course, costly, though much of it could be re-used when the garments themselves had been discarded. In 1664 Samuel Pepys gave to his wife's brother 'a coat that I had by me, a close-bodied, light-coloured coat, with a gold edgeing in each seam, that was the lace of my wife's best pettycoat, that she had when I married her'. Sprays and motifs might be cut away carefully from more worn-out parts to make a later reappearance as purses, pincushions and sweet-bags. Discretion was not, however, always observed in such matters: greatly to the amusement of his friends, that determined social and political climber of the 18th century, George Bubb Dodington, decorated his state bed at Eastbury with 'a carpeting of gold and silver embroidery which too glaringly betrayed its derivation from coat, waistcoat and breeches by the testimony of pockets, buttonholes and loops'.[1]

[1] *Molly Lepell*, by D. M. Stuart. Harrap, 1936.

The resident embroiderers that were employed in earlier centuries in most large households made extensive use of cords, not only in their costume embroideries, but for ornamenting chairs, stools, cushions, curtains and bed-hangings. While there are, of course, many decorative cords that can be plaited or knotted entirely with the fingers, others are better and more quickly made with the aid of some implement or mechanical device. In 1620 a French writer on needlework listed '*un rouet pour faire les cordons*' among the essential items of equipment for an embroiderer, and references to 'machines' or 'engines' for cord-making occur throughout the 18th century. An early and simple appliance of this kind may be seen in Plate 150. It consists of an iron clamp embodying a shaft at one end of which is a hook and at the other end a handle. The threads to be twisted were looped over the hook and held firmly at the far end while the handle was turned.

For making a three-ply twist a somewhat more elaborate device was employed. It consisted of three small, grooved wheels, each with a hook in the centre, mounted on a stand immediately above a larger and similar wheel to which they were connected by means of a string. The three threads, clamped at one end on to a table, were attached at the other end to the three hooks. The handle was then turned, causing the hooks to revolve, while the stand, steadied with the left hand, moved towards the clamp with the shortening of the threads. The object of this preliminary process was to increase the normal twist of the threads. As soon as they showed signs of curling up into loops, all three were placed on the top hook and the handle turned again, this time in the reverse direction. By this means they were twisted into a cord, which was kept tightly wound by the opposing tensions.

In the engraving reproduced from M. St Aubin's *L'Art du Brodeur*, published in 1770 (Plate 151), a cord-making implement of this kind, though slightly different in construction, may be seen; here four small wheels with hooks are geared to a larger wheel by means of cogs, the whole appliance being held in the hand, thus allowing for more freedom of movement.

Apart from the garniture of needlework there were numerous other purposes for which cords were needed in both large and small households. In medieval times horn-books, pen-cases, pincushions, pomanders and many objects of everyday use hung from the waist suspended by cords. Hooks and eyes and metal fasteners, of a type that can be bought easily and cheaply today, did not become generally available until the late Georgian era, so that both under and outer garments had to be laced up or gathered in with cords, or 'chains' as they were then termed. The closure of bags and purses presented another and more difficult problem; money was often carried in a silk purse contained in an outer bag of leather drawn up or tied round with strings or laces.

All these cords had, of course, to be made by hand, usually on a simple, but very essential, implement known as a lucet. This is a flat, lyre-shaped tool, from three to six inches in length, with two horns tapering or curved outwards at the ends (Plate 152). It produces a square, tightly-knotted cord that is extremely strong and does not stretch—points of considerable importance where tying or lacing are concerned. It will be seen that the base of the implement is so shaped that it can be revolved easily in the palm of the hand; alternatively it may be mounted on a handle that can be turned with the fingers (Plate 153), in which case it is sometimes referred to as a chain fork or, on the Continent, as a hay-fork, an implement which it certainly resembles. The method of making the cord (see Fig. 10) was as follows:

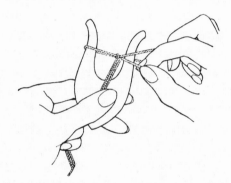

Fig. 10. Diagram showing the making of a lucetted cord

With the lucet held in the left hand and the ball of thread in the right, the end of the thread was passed through the hole in the base from back to front and secured in position with the left thumb. The thread was brought up at the back of the implement between the horns and wound in front of and then behind the right horn and, similarly, in front of and behind the left horn, in the manner of a figure eight, and was then brought out between the two horns. With the right thumb and fore-finger the loop round the right horn was loosened, slipped over the working thread and over the top of the horn, and the loop tightened. The lucet was next turned round in the hand, bringing the right horn forward, from right to left, the thread and knot being pulled across and tightened against what was now the right horn. With the thumb and fore-finger of the right hand the loop round this horn was loosened and the process continued as before, until the required length of cord was made.

At the end of the 18th century lucets were still in very general use; they were to be found in most cottages, often crudely shaped from horn or wood (left Plate 155), though for an elegant work-box they might be fashioned from ivory, pearl, or tortoiseshell with gold piqué. Those with a long handle sometimes have this hollowed out through the centre so that the cord can be passed through it and protrude from the end as with peg-knitting. An exceptionally large carved wooden lucet, mounted on a handle, is on view in the Hollytrees Mansion Museum, Colchester, and was probably used for upholstery. Mrs Boscowen, writing to her friend Mrs Delany in 1785, refers to a 'lucette footstool', and also to a 'carpet for the lucette', presumably trimmed or made with the cord.

When strong, machine-made cords and laces began to appear in shops, domestic cord-making went out of fashion, and by late Georgian times the lucet was already something of a curiosity. A periodical for young ladies dating from about 1830 states: 'A lucette is a small instrument something in the form of an Irish Harp, used for making little chains. As they can now, however, be had at a lower price than the silk required for making one costs, the lucette is very little used.' In some forms of needlework the tool may still be employed with advantage; to those entrusted with the repair of old costumes or ecclesiastical embroideries it may be of particular value. During a railway journey in Italy recently, a nun who had entered the carriage was seen to take a long-handled lucet from a pocket in the folds of her skirt and, revolving it in her hand with an ease and regularity born of long practice, kept her eyes firmly fixed upon the slowly lengthening cord until her journey was completed.

A tool that was also of great importance in earlier centuries, but which has lost much of its usefulness in modern days, is the stiletto. It will usually be found accompanying the lucet as it was needed for making the eyelet holes through which cords or laces could be threaded. Old stilettos are made from a variety of materials and are sometimes elaborately ornamented. Like many needlework tools they were worn hanging from the waist or were carried in the capacious pockets of 16th- and 17th-century dresses. In these circumstances some protection for the points was obviously necessary. If the implement was of metal an ornamental sheath was provided, but if of ivory it was generally made in two parts, the point being reversible and screwing into the handle when not in use.

One of the carved ivory implements in Plate 157 served a double purpose; here the point of the stiletto unscrews to disclose a metal pricker, for use in gold work and also for preparing patterns for pouncing on to material: the outlines of the design, drawn on parchment or paper, were pricked round at close intervals, placed on the fabric to be embroidered, and rubbed over with a pad containing fine graphite powder, or a white chalk pounce. A pricker was also essential for the maker of pillow lace in marking out the pattern to be followed.

With the gradual introduction of machine-made buttons and metal fastenings at the beginning of the 19th century the stiletto was no longer required for ordinary household sewing, apart from leather-work, though its importance had increased in another sphere. During the latter part of the 18th century there had arisen in this country a fashion for a form of work known as Eyelet-work and which today is known as Broderie Anglaise. In true Eyelet-work the pattern is composed entirely of round or oval eyelets, even the stalks of leaves and flowers being rendered in a succession of diminishing holes overcast in thread. For this type of embroidery the stiletto was, of course, essential, and though now less ornamental, and without the sheath that accompanied it in earlier years, it is always to be found in work-boxes of the Victorian era. A short, ivory stiletto may be attached to a chain at the other end of which is a pointed implement used for picking out the threads from the material in drawn thread work. There is also a small tool of metal or tortoise-shell pointed at both ends, which was used for a similar purpose (Plate 10).

In France and Holland during the 18th century there had arisen a fashion for heavily raised embroidery in which flowers and leaves were worked over with close stitching that was afterwards cut to form a tuft or pile. Sets of wooden gauges of different thicknesses could be obtained for this kind of work. The outline of a petal or leaf having been drawn or traced on to the material, a gauge was laid upon it and a row of stitches worked over it for the necessary length. The gauge was then withdrawn, placed close against the first row and the stitching repeated, this process continuing until the design was completely covered. With a sharp pair of scissors the rows of stitches were next cut through and the pile trimmed to the desired shape.

Directions for this type of embroidery are to be found in women's magazines of the early 19th century when the use of thick wool and a new and improved kind of gauge were recommended. This implement, curving up slightly at one end, had a keen knife blade set in it lengthwise at this extremity. When a row of stitching had been completed, the gauge was withdrawn, the knife blade cutting through the centre of the stitches, and thus ensuring an even pile.

Later in the century, when Berlin Patterns became readily available (*see* Chapter 15), many large pictures, from old masters to contemporary portraits, were copied entirely in raised work. Sets of identical gauges were employed, that could be worked over and left on the canvas until a number of rows had been completed. The stitching was then coated with gum on the reverse side, to fix it firmly in place, before the gauges were withdrawn. Pictures executed in this manner in France, where silk was often used instead of wool, have a surface that resembles closely shaved velvet.

About 1845 raised work was greatly simplified by the introduction of yet another type of gauge; this had a deep groove at one end into which a small blade could be inserted immediately before withdrawal. The danger of cutting the fingers while working was thus avoided.

. Birchwood box, lined blue silk,
ith pearl and silver fittings, made
r John Taylor of Tyrone, in 1820, as
n intended betrothal gift; the
ecoration is in pen-and-ink, partially
nted. His race horses are depicted
n the lid; on the front is a hunting
ene; on the sides, his greyhounds,
c. The artist, who signs himself
V'. is unknown.

95. (Left) Light tortoiseshell box with pearl decoration, lined pink and white satin. The fittings are of silver, ivory and tortoiseshell; a tray beneath holds writing implements and there are two secret drawers; 1810.

96. Typical early 19th-century Chinese lacquered box with bone fittings, and Christian name painted on inside of lid, made for sale to Europeans.

97. Saffian casket, lined pink satin, with set of cotton balls, and silver fittings dated 1831, commemorating the coronation of William IV and Adelaide.

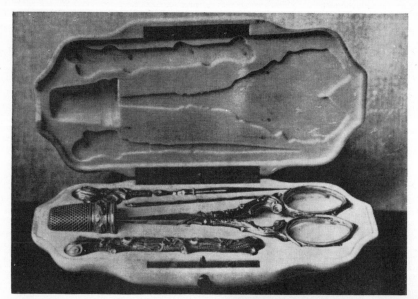

98. Early 19th-century sewing case, with silver-gilt fittings.

99. A Spanish walnut (with three-penny bit for scale) lined pink satin, and with gilt tray to hold gilt scissors, thimble, stiletto, bodkin and green glass needle-case; c. 1840.

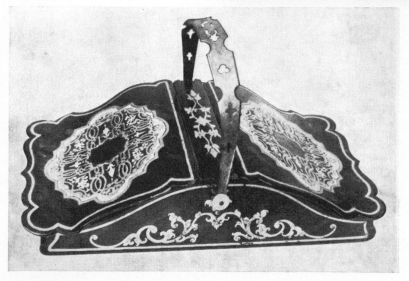

100. Papier-mâché basket-type work-box by Jennings and Bettridge; early 19th century.

101. Mahogany work-table with work-box below, attributed to Duncan Phyfe; New York, *c.* 1810.   102. Regency inlaid work- and games-table, with shallow drawer divided into compartments, and deep drawer beneath for holding work.

103. (Left) Victorian work-table with compartments surrounding a central tapering well for holding work.
104. Sewing case veneered to represent a barrel (closed and open); *c.* 1800.

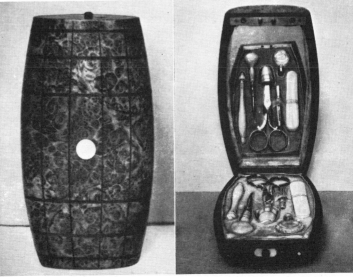

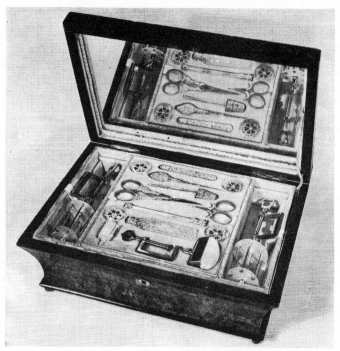

105. Veneered wooden box containing steel hemming clamp and a pair of steel winding clamps. The other fittings are richly mounted in gold; *c.* 1810.

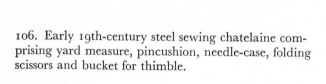

106. Early 19th-century steel sewing chatelaine comprising yard measure, pincushion, needle-case, folding scissors and bucket for thimble.

107. Louis XV chatelaine by Jean Ducrollay, Paris 1760. The nine fitted wood cases have engraved gold mounts and are suspended on gold chains. Thimble and needle-case are of gold; the *aide mémoire* has lacquer panels with gilt decoration.

108. *The Visit of the Angels* by the Master Bertram, *c.* 1390. Here the Madonna is seen picking up the stitches round the neck of a garment. The painting, formerly part of the altar of Buxtehude Abbey, Germany, is now in the Art Gallery, Hamburg.

109. (*left*) Cord knitted with hollow cork and four brass pegs. (*centre*) Wooden ring for peg-knitting. (*right*) Cord knitted on four loose sticks.

110. Ivory implement for knitting a loose girdle and a smaller ebony and ivory tube for knitting a finer cord.

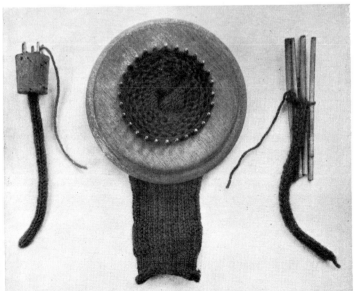

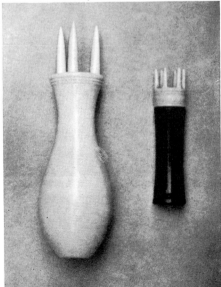

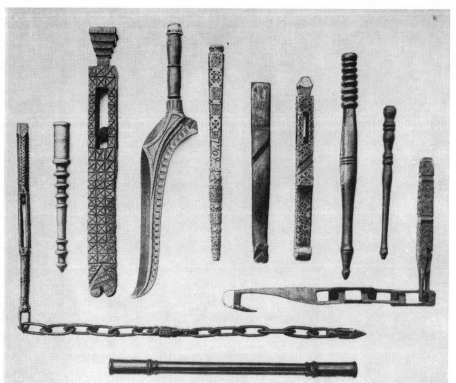

111. Wooden knitting sheaths, two with chain and tension hook; 18th and early 19th centuries. (*below*) Rosewood knitting-needle case with slit through which the work can protrude.

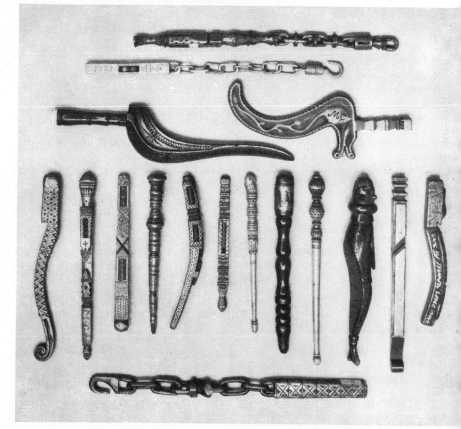

112. English and Continental knitting sheaths; 18th and 19th centuries. Of the vertical sheaths, the 3rd from the left contains a miniature hour glass; the 2nd and 5th have apron slots composed of two hearts; the 7th and 9th are of boxwood, French or Italian; the 10th is mahogany, carved in the form of a walrus.

113. Continental
boxwood knitting
sheaths; 17th and
18th centuries.

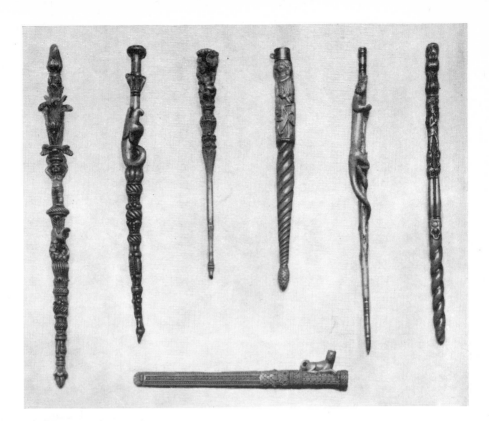

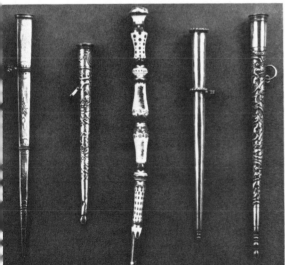

114. Four Continental knitting sheaths, and
(*centre*) porcelain sheath with coloured and gilt
decoration.

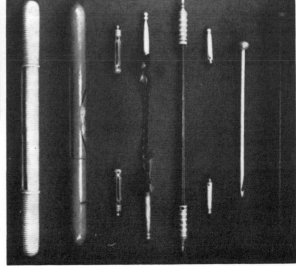

115. (*left*) Ivory and wood knitting-needle cases,
with slit for work to protrude, the larger 10″ in
length. (*centre*) Four sets of ivory and bone needle
protectors. (*right*) Two hooks with knobs, for
tricot crochet.

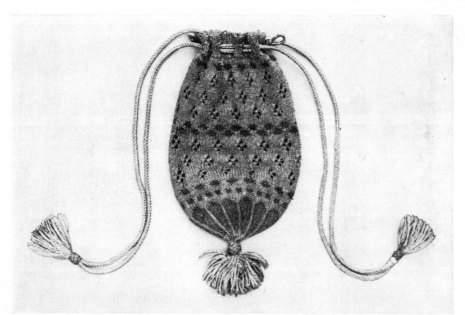

116. Purse knitted in
orange silk and silver
thread, drawn up
with lucetted cords;
early 17th century.

117. Box covered with fine bead-knitting; 18th century.

118. Mat knitted in fine white cotton;
early 19th century.

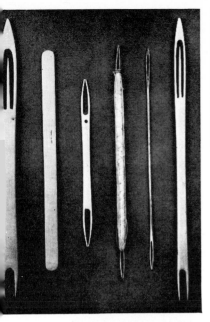

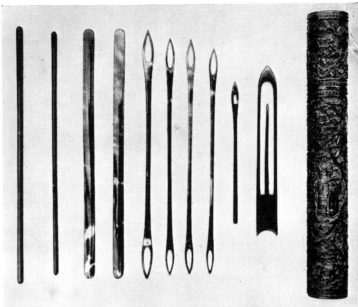

119. (*left and right*) Two large single-ended wooden netting-needles; a bone gauge and needle, and two steel needles, one filled with thread having criss-cross winding, to keep strands in place.

120. Netting tools and case, carved from tortoiseshell; 18th century.

121. Straw-work netting-box in the form of a book, and two straw-work cases for netting implements.

122. The netting-box open.

123. (Left) Engraving after Moreau
le Jeune. The woman on the right
is netting with a device similar to the
one shown in Plate 122; *c.* 1776.

124. *Miss Elizabeth Wheatley, netting,* by Francis
Alleyne (1750-1815).

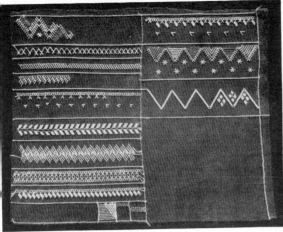

125. (Left) Early 19th-century sampler of darning stitches on machine-made net.

126. (Right) Hand-made and embroidered net; German, c. 1800.

127. (Left) Small netted mat with pattern produced by the use of different gauges. (*right*) Similar mat with darning at points; early 19th century.

128. Tablet for use in making Teneriffe or Brazilian Lace, diameter 10″; the special needle has a curved tip.

129. Late Georgian baby-caps. Machine-made net with hand embroidery.

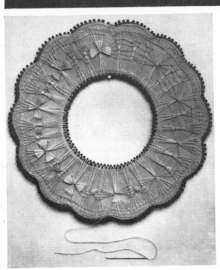

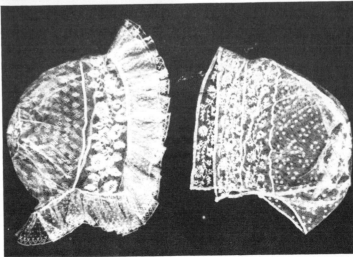

130. Teneriffe or Brazilian Lace; the inscription *Viva Mexico* surrounds the Mexican Eagle with Snake.

131. Finely worked Teneriffe Lace. The diameter of the smaller circles forming the edging is $1\frac{1}{4}''$.

132. Needle-made lace, a development from reticella work, still basically composed of buttonhole stitching but without the geometrical background of threads.

133. (Above) Italian reticella work (depth $4\frac{1}{2}''$). The linen foundation is visible at the edges. The pattern is built up with buttonhole stitching on threads stretched at intervals of $1''$.

134. (Left) *Lacis* or *filet* lace. The pattern is composed of simple darning stitches on hand-made net.

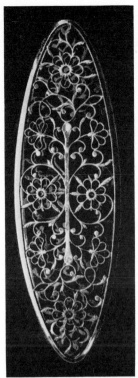

135. Silver filigree knotting shuttle.

136. Tortoiseshell knotting shuttle with inlay of embossed and chased decoration in silver and coloured golds; French, 18th century.

137. Large pierced and cut steel knotting shuttle; 18th century.

138. French 18th-century knotting shuttle, chiselled steel, parcel gilt.

139. Linen doublet, *c.* 1630, with knotted linen cords couched to the fabric and interspersed with French knots in linen thread.

140. *Madame Danger, knotting*, by Louis le Tocqué (1696–1772).

141. Two knotting shuttles; one French, painted wood; the other Chinese, carved ivory.   142. (*left and right*) Large tortoiseshell knotting shuttles, one with gold piqué. (*centre*) Tortoiseshell knotting shuttle, with silver piqué decoration; two tatting shuttles, the larger of horn inlaid with shell.

143. Ivory knotting shuttle stained rose pink, $4\frac{1}{2}''$. Five tatting shuttles; two oriental ivory, one Tunbridge ware, one mother-of-pearl and one silver. Gold tatting-pin on chain.

144. Mother-of-pearl tatting shuttle and gauge.

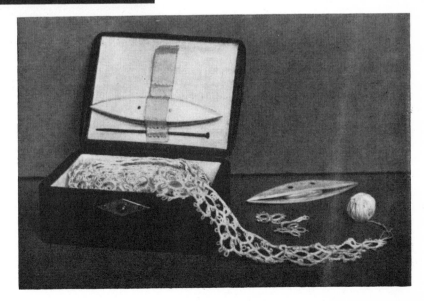

145. Leather covered tatting box with two shuttles and purling pin.

146. *The Countess of Albemarle, knotting,* by Sir Joshua Reynolds, 1750. The open end of the knotting shuttle can be clearly seen. 147. *Marie-Adélaide de France,* by Nattier (1685–1766). The close knotting of the thread can be seen between the left hand and the knotting bag.

148. Tatting, or *Occhi,* so-called from the 'eyes' of which it is composed.

12

Tambouring and Crochet

CROCHET, as we know it today, was introduced into this country in the first quarter of the 19th century and, though ancient in origin, it is the most recently developed of all established forms of needlework. There can be little doubt that its history is as old as that of knitting to which it is closely allied; but while knitting, owing to its greater speed and the elasticity of the fabric it produced, was put to a wide variety of uses, crochet emerged only slowly. In the wardrobe accounts of Edward IV, in 1480, there is a reference to payments made to Piers Draper, citizen and ironmonger, for 'crochets of the most and myddel and leeste assise'. From the fact that these are mentioned in the same sentence as tapehooks and tenterhooks, used in weaving, it is reasonable to assume that they were connected with needlework; but, as the word crochet was sometimes used for a hairpin, early references must be read with some reserve.

In the 18th century in this country embroidering with the aid of a hook was known as tambouring, but it differed from modern crochet, as it was then used for ornamenting the surface of materials, not for making trimmings or articles that were entire in themselves. It was called tambouring because in the East, where it originated, the fabric to be decorated was stretched tightly on a frame resembling a tambour or drum (Fig. 11).

The hook, or tambouring needle as it is sometimes termed, was similar to a metal crochet hook, though sharper and set in a handle broadening towards the top, to provide a firm grip for the fingers. The embroiderer held it in a vertical position in the right hand and inserted it downward through the material stretched on the frame, where it picked up the thread held underneath in the left hand, and drew it in a loop to the upper surface of the fabric, in such a manner that each succeeding loop held down the one previously made, thus producing a chain stitch. By this means patterns could be outlined, or filled in, at much greater speed than when worked in a chain stitch made with an ordinary needle.

The tambour allowed for the free movement of the hands above and below the material, which is necessary when working with a hook; it was also a convenient shape for resting between the knees when sitting cross-legged on the ground, a position commonly assumed in the East. In the West the tambour was usually supported on a wooden stand (Plate 151) and, eventually, the curved base, found to be cumbersome, was entirely discarded, the essential circular top alone being retained.

Tambouring has another characteristic which distinguishes it from most other forms of surface embroidery; it requires a long, continuous thread which must flow freely and evenly as it is drawn up to the underside of the work. In Chardin's painting *La Mère Laborieuse* (Plate 158) the woman who is seated, with a tambour hoop resting against her knee, is drawing the thread

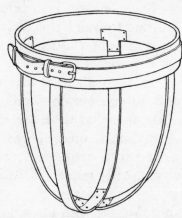

Fig. 11. Old tambour frame, of the original form from which the name is derived.

direct from a box-shaped skein holder which revolves slowly as she pulls out the yarn. Where the tambour hoop was mounted on a stand, a reel fixed immediately beneath it was frequently provided for holding the thread (Plate 160).

A much more elegant device was the ornamental tambouring reel-holder which was worn by nearly every woman of fashion who owned a tambour hoop at the latter end of the 18th century (Plates 161 and 162). The reel itself, of bone or ivory and about four inches in width, revolved on the spindle of the holder which hung by a short chain from an ornamental clasp fitting over the waistbelt, thus holding the thread in a convenient position near the underside of the work. The holder might be semi-circular or square shouldered and was often elaborately decorated in keeping with the graceful dresses of the period.

When embroidering a large piece of material, the tambour hoop had its disadvantages as its position had continually to be moved. In time, therefore, a wider, rectangular frame was devised, mounted on a stand, with a roller and ratchet at either end between which the material was stretched horizontally, the work, as it progressed, being wound from one roller to the other. In the Frontispiece Madame de Pompadour may be seen seated at one of these frames, the needle in her right hand while her left hand guides the thread. As this portrait must have been painted before 1764, the year in which she died, it is obvious that in France tambour-work was well developed by the middle of the 18th century.

In these islands also tambouring had become extremely popular. The easy, free-flowing lines of the chain stitch were found to be as effective when worked in fine thread on the most delicate muslin as they were in silk, metal or woollen threads used with heavier stuffs. H. G. Graham, in his *Social Life in Scotland in the 18th Century*, speaks of girls and women in country society in the earlier half of the century 'deft with their fingers at sewing cambric or plying their tambouring'. In *The School for Scandal*, published in 1777, Sir Peter Teazle reminds his wife that she was once 'the daughter of a plain country squire . . . when I saw you first sitting at your tambour'. John Byng the diarist, writing of a visit he had paid to Farnham Castle in 1782, complains that the building lacked the dignity of an episcopal residence: the petticoat, he states, rules the cassock, 'for the long gallery is furnished with modern frippery such as tambour-frames'.

There is, nevertheless, one difficulty here: in these early references it is by no means always certain what is meant by the word tambouring, as the term becomes very loosely applied to other forms of embroidery for which a tambour frame was found to be equally suitable. Sylas Neville noted in his diary that at a Jewish wedding which he attended in 1782 'a canopy of white satin with tambour-work was held over the bride and bridegroom'. Even with his keen eye for detail it is unlikely that he was describing some particular stitch but was referring rather to embroidery in general terms. The 'tambour waistcoat' that was worn by most fashionably dressed men, and often mentioned in letters and journals of this period, may, or may not, have been embroidered with a tambour hook.

That the work reached the height of its popularity here at the end of the 18th century there can be no doubt, particularly for the embroidery of fine muslin (Plate 168). The tools needed for this delicate stitching are to be found in many an old work-box. The most elegant of these implements are turned from ivory or shell, no thicker at their widest part than an ordinary pencil (Plates 163 and 11). The stouter half of the handle unscrews to reveal within its hollow interior five or six metal hooks in graded sizes. There is a winged screw at one side to secure the hook in position; the long, pointed cap that protects the hook, when not in use, can be screwed on to the top of the handle. Ivory tambour hooks of this type are sometimes mounted with gold (Plate 154); others are fashioned from bone with elaborate lathe turning.

Tambouring became commercialised in the 1780s, particularly in Scotland, where fine muslin was embroidered in quantity by girls seated round large rectangular frames made specially for this purpose; but in the late Georgian era, when it was found that the stitch could be quickly and perfectly produced by mechanical means, this type of hand embroidery fell out of favour.

Meanwhile, in France at the end of the 18th century, the work, which was there known as crochet (having taken its name from the hook rather than from the frame), was undergoing a gradual change. Instead of being employed for surface embroidery, the hook was now used for making a series of chain stitches looped into one another in such a manner that they formed complete and independent edgings and insertions that could be utilised in the same way as lace. This method of working, to which the French gave the appropriate name of '*crochet en air*,' is the crochet that we know today.

How far the existence of the tambour hook was responsible for its development it is difficult to determine for, original as it may have seemed to most people at the time, 'crochet in the air' was by no means new. It was known in Italy and the adjacent countries in the 16th century, though the fact that it had acquired the name of 'Nuns' Lace' suggests that, like many other forms of needlework, it was practised mainly in religious houses; the old, ivory hooks in Plate 115 may well have been intended for use in a convent. By the end of the 18th century the technique of crochet had become well established in Spain; the silver-gilt donkeys in Plate 164, which are Spanish in origin and date from this period, carry a set of hooks, with a handle, in their panniers. The hooks here, it will be noticed, are bent round in a simple crook.

In this country fine crochet was little known before 1820. It was developed and popularised by a woman of Franco-Spanish descent, Mlle Eleanore Riego de la Branchardière, the daughter of a nobleman who had fled to this country at the time of the French Revolution. Having visited the nuns of the Blackrock Convent in Dublin where, it is probable, some of the older designs for crochet had been preserved, she devoted herself to the further development of the work, building up the most complicated patterns with the use of metal hooks and fine thread. She not only taught her art to several members of the English Royal Family, but, from 1852 to 1854, produced a monthly journal of her own called *The Needle*, and wrote, in all, about 100 books on needlework. Her patterns for crochet remained in use for over a century.

The hooks employed in this type of work were similar to those needed for tambouring and, at first, like tambour hooks, they were made in sets of graded sizes, though the handles into which they were screwed might be straight instead of broadening towards the top, as they were intended to be held horizontally, not vertically. Flat, tortoiseshell boxes, resembling card cases, may contain either tambour or crochet hooks (Plate 165). By the middle of the century the winged screw at the side of the handle had been replaced by a metal fitting similar to a modern drill chuck. Cylindrical boxes of bone or ivory, or veneered with mother-of-pearl, were also made for holding crochet hooks; in Scotland they were often turned from wood and painted in tartan patterns. A particularly interesting crochet hook case is illustrated in the centre of Plate 165. It is solidly constructed of synthetic ivory and ebony to represent a railway engine, the 'boiler' containing a central hole for the handle, with holes for six hooks ranged round it. This is not a toy for a child; it was made at a time when, even to an adult, a railway engine was a new and fascinating object.

In addition to these fine metal hooks, larger hooks of wood, bone, ivory or tortoiseshell, of varying lengths and proportions, are also to be found in old work-boxes. These may be more difficult to date as they were intended for wool crochet which has a very different history. Wool crochet did not develop originally as a form of embroidery; it arose independently among the wool-growing communities in those parts of the world where the severity of the climate made the production of warm and useful garments of primary importance. The work in these early days was regarded as a form of knitting, and in this respect the following passage from *The Memoirs of a Highland Lady*, by Elizabeth Grant, is of particular relevance. It concerns a visit that she paid in the year 1812 to her great-grand-uncle, Captain Lewis Grant, at Inverdruie:

'Sometimes when he was not well he wore a plaid cloak, and a night-cap, red or white, made by his industrious wife in a stitch she called shepherd's knitting; it was done with a little hook which she manufactured for herself out of the tooth of an old tortoiseshell comb, and she used to go on looping her home-spun wool as quickly as fingers could move, making not only caps, but drawers and waistcoats for winter wear for the old husband she took such care of.'

It is clear from this account that the method of working which we now call crochet, though unknown in most parts of this country at the beginning of the last century, was by no means unfamiliar in the Scottish Highlands and that, as the hook used was home-made, such implements were not ordinarily obtainable. That Mrs Grant should have referred to her work as shepherd's knitting is also significant, for it indicates that by the cottagers, in whose families it had most likely been handed down through countless generations, it was still regarded as a form of knitting. It was not until many years later that Mlle Riego began to publish her books on crochet and, while she may justly claim to have 'invented' some of the elaborate patterns of the Victorian era, she also seems to have been well aware of the earlier origins of crochet in its simplest form. In her instruction booklets she describes the first stitch that a beginner must master as 'single crochet or shepherd's knitting'.

A further instance of the close connection between knitting and crochet which has existed through the centuries is to be found in an Eastern form of the work, known in this country as Tunisian crochet. The hook used is stout, long and of uniform thickness, and is easily distinguished by the knob at one end (Plate 115). This knob is necessary to prevent the stitches from slipping off for, after the preliminary chain has been made, they are picked up one by one on to the shaft of the hook. In the second row, working backwards, the thread is put over the hook and drawn through each pair of stitches in turn until all have been cast off. With these two alternating rows of picking-up and casting-off a firm fabric is produced closely resembling knitting—the work is, in fact, sometimes known as tricot crochet. It was used in this country in the Victorian era for making mats and counterpanes, strips or squares of the crochet being worked separately and then joined together.

An implement used in conjunction with a crochet hook, familiar in former times but now comparatively rare, is the two-pronged fork employed in hairpin-work (Plate 166). In appearance the tool closely resembles the lucet; indeed, it must be obvious to anyone who is accustomed to lucetting that it was from this that hairpin-work derived. The implement is in both cases held and revolved in the palm of the hand, though in hairpin-work the loops, formed with the aid of a crochet hook, are not tightened but remain on the fork in a double row. When a number of loops have been formed, they are slipped off to make room for more, until a strip of the required length has been completed. The strip is then joined up, or combined with ordinary crochet in such a manner that an insertion or trimming is formed; examples of this very ingenious work may be seen in Plates 167 and 169. Old forks are made of wood, bone or ivory and, like the lucet, may have a handle (Plate 155); those of more recent date are of steel wire, turned round in a simple curve.

Although popular in Victorian days, hairpin-work is now seldom seen here, but is better known in France and Italy where, instead of the older fork, knitting needles are frequently used. They are secured in place by means of a regulator: a device consisting of two narrow metal plates fitting over one another and connected by screws. The needles, held vertically at the required distance apart, are slipped between the plates and when the screws are tightened are secured firmly in position. This invention has distinct advantages, as the space between the needles can be so easily adjusted for making strips of different widths.

For making a three- or four-tiered fringe in hairpin-work, a wooden implement known as a fringing-fork was used, consisting of one narrow and three or four wider prongs (Plate 155). It was held in the hand in the same manner as for ordinary hairpin crochet; the small loops, made on the one side by putting the thread round the narrow prong, constituted the heading, while the larger loops, formed by taking the thread in succession round the wider prongs, composed the fringe which hung down in several tiers when taken off the fork.

A form of work of Eastern origin, which it is thought may have had its origin in tambouring, though so very different in character, is the type of rug-making in which short lengths of yarn, or woollen material cut into strips, are looped into a background of coarse linen or burlap in such a manner that the loops stand up in a close, short pile. There are, in the main, two ways in which this can be done: by punching the wool downward through the material with a skewer or brod, in which case it is known as pegging or brodding; or by knotting the wool into the material with a hook. This latter method of working is well known to seamen who, from very early times, have made rugs and mats by looping lengths of rope into canvas; the hooks fashioned for this purpose often being found among sailors' sewing tools.

At the beginning of this century these pegged or hooked rugs were to be seen in nearly every cottage in this country and on the kitchen hearths of many larger houses. In some instances the loops of the pile were left uncut, in others they were sheared when the work was completed. In Scotland and some of the northern counties of England odd lengths of wool left over from weaving and known as 'thrums' were often used, but elsewhere strips of cloth cut from outworn garments usually sufficed, the sombre black and grey tones of everyday clothing that were the most easily procurable being relieved here and there by the bright scarlet cloth of an old military jacket or pink hunting coat. The patterns followed were simple and conventional, with little attempt at originality, and, with few exceptions, neither the rugs nor the tools with which they were made have been considered worth preserving.

In America, however, the story of hooked-rug making is very different. Introduced in the early days of colonisation, it developed into one of the most elaborate and decorative of all homely crafts. By the skilful dyeing and blending of colours, the use of many original designs, and the adaptation of traditional patterns from a wide variety of sources, a large number of very fine rugs were produced which are now much sought after by collectors. There is an extensive literature on the subject, tracing its history back to Coptic times, and detailing the different characteristics of the designs and hooks that are peculiar to the different States.

13

Purse-making, Beadwork, Braid- and Mat-weaving

THERE HAVE BEEN many previous references in this book to purse-making which, until the latter part of the 19th century, was an important branch of domestic needlework, involving netting, knitting and, eventually, crochet. Before the introduction of inexpensive metal frames and snap fastenings, such as are common at the present day, the problem of finding some convenient method of carrying money for everyday use was a very real one. The usual small pouch or bag, tied round or drawn up with cord, had never proved entirely satisfactory, as it did not allow for the separation of copper coins from those of greater value. Many people therefore carried two types of purse: one for pence and the other for gold or silver (Fig. 12). The copper purse, sometimes known as a pence-jug, consisted of a small bag of leather or stout

Fig. 12. (*left*) Pence jug or copper purse. (*right*) Gold and silver purse with flap raised; the coins were taken out from between the loosened threads.

linen, narrowing towards the top before broadening out to form a wide mouth. It had a handle attached at one side, and on to this a ring was threaded that could be slipped over the top and on to the neck of the purse, thus keeping the coins safely in place. A more elegant pence-jug, for a lady, might be knitted in silk thread.

Purses for gold and silver were also knitted, usually in a long strip that was folded over and sewn up in the shape of an elongated envelope, about two inches wide and three inches in depth, a short piece being left to form the flap. Four or more short strings were sewn at equal distances along the front edge of the opening and taken through the purse at the same level along the crease where the flap turned over. These strings were then gathered together and attached to a ring that could be slipped on to the finger if the purse was carried in the hand or, for safety when travelling, could be suspended from a cord worn round the neck and concealed within the clothing; the weight of the coins, in either case, kept the strings taut and the mouth of the purse firmly closed. When money was needed, the flap of the purse was lifted and the strings loosened with the fingers, so that the coins could be taken out from between them. It is from such a custom that the phrase 'to keep a tight hold on the purse strings' derives.

In Tudor days silk purses are mentioned in connection with the customary exchange of gifts between sovereigns and their subjects, and between officials of high rank, on New Year's Day and other great festivals. There was a regulated scale of values to be observed at such times, by both giver and receiver, and custom demanded that gifts of money should be presented in a manner worthy of the occasion. In 1561 the Earl of Bedford gave to the Queen £20 in gold 'in a purse of black silk and gold knit', and his Countess £10 in gold in a similar purse of crimson silk and silver thread.[1] As under these circumstances the purses were not intended for everyday use, safe closure was of less importance, and they might take the form of small bags drawn up in the ordinary way with cord or ribbon, such as the example in Plate 116, which is knitted in orange silk and silver thread.

Many of these small purses were made by means of a specially constructed device such as that seen on the right of Plate 170. The method employed was that of peg-knitting, described in Chapter 8. The implement was known as a Purse-mould, or sometimes as a *Moule Turc*, an indication of the Eastern origin of this form of work; but the word 'mould' here is somewhat misleading as it is, of course, merely a ring for knitting a tube, with a base conveniently shaped to the grasp of the hand. On the left of this same plate is a hollow, thimble-shaped implement entirely different from the *Moule Turc*, but also known as a Purse-mould. It is of thin wood, with two rows of holes running in shallow grooves near the top. The term 'mould' in this instance was used with justification for the purse, worked with needle and thread, was shaped to its outer contour (see Plate 173).

To make a simple purse in silk on a thimble-mould only one row of holes

[1] Gladys Scott Thomson, *Two Centuries of Family History*. Longmans, 1930.

was used. A needle was threaded with a long length of silk of the required colour with a large knot at one end. This knot was held down with the left thumb on the outside of the mould, near the top, while the silk was wound once round the groove immediately over the row of holes. The needle was then taken through the knot, and the silk wound once again round the mould, this time in the opposite direction to tighten the thread, after which it was secured by working one or two buttonhole stitches into the knot. Needle and silk were then left hanging. Another needle, with a length of tacking thread having a large knot at the end, was then passed through one of the holes from the inside of the mould to the outside, over the silk threads, and back through the same hole, this process being continued until the silk was firmly secured all round the mould, thus forming a firm foundation for the rim of the purse.

Returning to the needle and silk left hanging, a row of stitches was now worked *à feston* over the silk threads. These were simply buttonhole stitches left loose, instead of being tightened, and by working each successive row into the loops of the one above it the purse was built up, the number of stitches being gradually reduced towards the base, to fit the curve of the mould. Finally, the tacking thread round the rim was cut and the purse released.

The buttonhole stitch, *à feston*, described here, is the first and simplest stitch used in needlepoint lace. There are numerous variations of it, many of a much more elaborate character, and by the use of two needles and different coloured silks, with the added introduction of gold and silver threads, purses of a most decorative kind could be made. Alternatively, beads could be introduced; the purse in Plate 173, to which reference has already been made, is worked *à feston* in beads of several colours and lined with yellow gauze. Here, as so often in past centuries, the closure of the top has presented a problem, but it has been solved by attaching a series of long threads at regular intervals to the rim and threading them through a large bead that could be moved up and down as required. Descriptions of this method of purse-making are sometimes to be found in books on domestic occupations and amusements for young ladies in the early Victorian period, but, in fact, with the advent of the more practical wallet-purse in the latter half of the 18th century, the wooden, thimble-shaped moulds had already been discarded. Today they are extremely rare.

The wallet-purse, sometimes called a stocking- or miser-purse, consisted of a long tubular bag sewn up at the ends, and with a narrow longitudinal slit in the middle forming the opening (Plate 172). Two small rings were passed over the bag, gathering it in towards the centre, and a tassel, weighted with beads, was attached at each end. When the two rings were drawn to one side of the opening money could be inserted through the central slit and secured in place by drawing one of the rings across towards that extremity of the bag; copper coins were kept in one end and gold and silver in the other, different coloured beads distinguishing the two compartments. A large number of 18th-century wallet-purses were netted, but later knitting and crochet became popular as they allowed for more extensive bead decoration. The rectangular boxes with roller and ratchet, described in Chapter 9, were often known as purse-netting boxes though they were not intended specifically for this purpose. They sometimes contain flat wooden moulds over which the purses were tacked or sewn up at the side and ends (Plate 172).

To fix the stitches more firmly in their relative positions, and to ensure that the purse should retain its correct shape, a specially designed purse-stretcher was employed (Fig. 13). It was composed of two pieces of wood which when placed together, formed a cylinder; when not in use they could be joined by means of two hooks and pins. At each end of one of the pieces of wood a

Fig. 13. Purse stretcher, used in making wallet purses.

hole was bored to take a long, blunt-ended screw. The purse, when finished, but before the ends were drawn up, was tacked up at the mouth and passed over the cylinder. It was then damped, and the screws were inserted and tightened. After remaining on the stretcher for some hours it was removed, the tacking stitches were cut, and the rings and tassels added.

Wallet-purses were equally popular with both sexes. Women held them in the palms of their hands when shopping, the two ends hanging down on either side; men carried them in their pockets. William Cowper was inspired, on one occasion, to write a graceful lyric of twelve lines to his cousin, Anne Bodham, 'on receiving from her a network purse made by herself'. On the other hand, Lord Bessborough, writing to the Ladies of Llangollen in 1781, has no hesitation in making the following request to Sarah Ponsonby: 'I desire the favour of you not to send me the Purse you mention, for I have, I believe, twenty by me which are not of any use. It has been the fashion of ladies to make purses and they have been so obliging as to give me a great many.'

This fashion had in no way abated at the beginning of the 19th century, for Elizabeth Grant, giving an account of a visit to Lord Lauderdale's at Dunbar in 1817, describes the ladies as busily engaged 'netting purses'.

Catherine Hutton, daughter of the Birmingham historian, who was born in 1756, recalled at the end of her long life that she had 'netted upwards of one hundred wallet purses'.

In the 17th and 18th centuries reference is sometimes made to small purses of 'silk rybben'. These were not meant to withstand everyday wear and tear, but were used by both men and women on social occasions, particularly as gaming purses (Plate 174). They were usually made from several yards of silk ribbon of two different colours, and, again, the use of a mould was involved. In this instance it consisted of a square of thin wood or stiff cardboard over which the two lengths of ribbon were wound and interwoven diagonally. When the mould was completely enclosed, the ribbon was secured by a line of stitches a short distance below what was to be the top edge. A pair of scissors was then inserted and the purse cut open above the row of stitches so that the mould could be withdrawn. The raw edges were afterwards bound over and a draw-string threaded through.

It was evidently this type of purse that Parson Woodforde used for holding the shillings and sixpences that he won or lost at his nightly game of cards with his niece, Nancy, or with Squire Custance and his Lady, for an entry in his diary in October, 1784, reads: 'For 5 yards of Orange and Purple or rather Blue Ribband for a purse for myself pd. 2/6d.' The method of making such a purse, probably Chinese in origin, is extremely ingenious: there is an exact relation to be observed between the width of the ribbon and the size of the mould. For the example illustrated in Plate 174, for instance, which is three inches square, a ribbon three-eighths of an inch wide must be used.

Beadwork, far commoner in the more leisurely days of the past than it is at the present time, was introduced in a variety of ways into purse-making. The small silk purse on the left of Plate 174 is composed of ordinary knitting combined with bead knitting, that in Plate 171 of beaded crochet with a bead crochet base, and that in Plate 175 of bead knitting with a silk crochet top; the beads had, of course, to be strung on to the thread in the right order before work commenced. It will be noticed that ornamentation is not the sole object here; in each instance the beads give added strength to the base of the purse which takes the wear and tear and weight of the coins.

A pastime that delighted the ladies of the 17th century was threading beads of appropriate colours on to wire, and by twisting, padding and stitching, forming them into the shapes of fruit, flowers and even miniature gardens. This type of ornamentation is closely associated with stump work, and is also to be seen on the beadwork trays or layette baskets that were made as christening gifts in the Stuart period. A similar method of working was employed in decorating the 18th-century tubular needlecases shown in Plate 6; the beads here were strung on to a length of wire or silk which was then wound round a slender case turned from wood or bone, each row being attached to the previous one by buttonhole or other stitching.

For embroidery on canvas, often in conjunction with silk or wool work, the beads had to be taken up one by one with the needle and sewn down separately. This same method was formerly used when beading materials in costume embroidery, always a lengthy and costly procedure. In modern bead embroidery, however, the needle has been discarded in favour of the tambour hook—a singular instance of a new use having been found for an old tool. In tambour-beading the beads are strung on to the working thread beforehand; they are then moved up one by one and secured to the material by means of the hook, the chain stitch appearing on the wrong side of the work (see Chapter 12).

Indian beadwork, so called because it originated among the Apache Indians of Arizona and New Mexico, but later introduced into European countries, requires a very different technique as well as a specially constructed loom (Plate 177). The warp threads, attached at one end to a roller, and fixed at the other end with pegs, are stretched over two upright pieces of wood along each of which is a series of notches. In these notches the threads lie at regular intervals. One end of the working thread, having been tied on to the warp thread farthest to the left, is then threaded through a long, very fine needle and the beads needed for one row strung on to it. Needle and thread are next brought underneath the warp, where the beads are pressed upwards with the fingers so that each one lies between two threads. The needle is then pushed through the beads from right to left, this time on top of the warp, thus securing them in position. The main advantage of this method of working is that the two sides of the beadwork are identical; it was therefore found particularly suitable for making articles such as girdles, bracelets, necklaces and hand-screens (Plate 176).

The most delicate beadwork dates from the last quarter of the 18th century when, following advances in the technique of glass manufacture, beads of almost incredible fineness, of sparkling crystal and bright, translucent colours became available. They were imported into this country from Venice, and from Gablonz in Bohemia. They were always costly and, when towards the middle of the last century beadwork became a popular pastime, they were displaced by larger, more crudely made beads of opaque colours that could be obtained in quantity at a very low price.

There are a number of small looms which, from the manner of their use, belong rather to the sphere of needlework than to that of weaving. Like the Apache loom they have a roller and ratchet at one end, and some simple device for fixing the warp threads at regular intervals. They date from the latter part of the 18th century, and were known as braid looms, as they were intended mainly for weaving braids and ribbons (Plate 179). Most of them are well made and highly finished, occasionally with a decorative inlay. In some examples there is a roller at both ends and a heddle for raising and lowering alternate threads of the warp, but, as a rule, the weaving was done with an ordinary needle and thread worked in and out, backwards and forwards, as the pattern demanded; in this way, with the use of different coloured silks, various designs could be followed.

Braid weaving remained an engaging drawing-room occupation until about 1825, when, following the introduction of the Jacquard loom, pattern weaving by mechanical methods became possible. By 1830 the ribbon-weavers of Coventry were reproducing multi-coloured designs of all types, speedily and in quantity, and gaily patterned silk ribbons appeared in the shops at comparatively little cost.

A simple type of weaving, usually known as frame-work, was used for making shawls, mats and other household articles, though for such purposes only a very elementary device was needed. It consisted of a frame, from three to nine inches square, closely set round with pegs or pins about an inch in height, and in this last respect was very similar in appearance to the rings or frames used in peg-knitting. To make a shawl the wool was wound backwards and forwards, across the frame, round opposite pairs of pegs, either vertically and then horizontally, or diagonally, according to the type of pattern required. The weaving was done with a long needle approximately the same length as the frame. When a sufficient number of squares had been woven, they were sewn together or joined with openwork stitching; by the additional use of triangular frames geometrical patterns could be built up from the differently shaped pieces.

Although it has long gone out of fashion, frame-work, which is undoubtedly very ancient in origin, had its advantages, particularly when using up odd balls of wool, as even when the threads were not of uniform thickness the size of the square remained the same, a result that cannot so easily be ensured with knitting or crochet.

Mat-making could be a much more complicated process, although the same type of frame was used; in this case different coloured wools were generally chosen for the base and the surface. To commence, the wool for the base was attached to the peg at the left bottom corner; working from left to right, it was then taken in front of the next peg, across the frame and round the opposite peg and back, three times in all. This winding, three times round each pair of pegs, was continued along the entire row. With a half turn of the frame, the wool was taken round the pegs in the same manner until there were two layers of three strands running in either direction across the frame. The wool of the second colour was next attached to the corner peg exactly as before, and the whole process repeated. With an ordinary needle and a long thread the strands of wool were now firmly secured at each intersection with a cross stitch, the thread being carried along underneath the mat to the next crossing. This being done, the two top layers of wool were cut through exactly half way between each intersection, forming a series of tufts, leaving the wool of the other colour to form the base. The mat was then taken off the frame. The winding could be done diagonally as well as horizontally, and in silk or cotton if preferred.

Pillow Lace

THE WEAVER, on removing his work from the loom, finds, at each end of the fabric he has woven, a fringe formed by the unused extremities of the warp threads. These threads are usually sheared off and discarded, leaving a raw edge to be secured later with stitching; or, where rugs and carpets are concerned, they may be tied together in groups and cut off to form a short knotted fringe. In more primitive times the weavers of the Eastern countries, unwilling to waste any of their yarn, soon devised a method by which they could make use of the full length of these loose threads. By repeated twisting and knotting, with their fingers, they plaited them into deep borders that were not only ornamental but added length and weight to shawls, towels, window-blinds and other domestic objects.

So effective was this work found to be that, in the course of time, it developed into a household craft independent of weaving; strips and fringes that were entire in themselves were made in varying widths to be inserted in, or added to, fabrics of different kinds, as and when required; while long lengths of thread, often of gold or silver, were twisted into narrow braids or 'laces' that could be used in embroidery. For such a method of working, a pillow or padded board was used, across which a horizontal thread could be stretched taut and secured at each end with a pin. To this horizontal thread the vertical threads were then tied and allowed to hang down over the front of the pillow where they could be picked up more easily with the tips of the fingers and plaited or knotted into the required pattern.

The work, which is extremely ancient in origin, spread from the Near East into Southern Europe where it was known as Macramé or Macrami, terms derived from the Turkish word *magrama*, a towel. It was also known as Mexican Lace, having presumably been introduced into South America by the Spaniards who had learned the art from the Moors.

In this country in the 17th and 18th centuries there is occasional mention of 'machines' or 'engines' for knotting fringes; these were frames or clamps of various kinds, for supporting the main horizontal thread, which were now taking the place of the earlier pillow. By late Georgian times knotted-fringe work had become a popular drawing-room pastime and, as a coarse thread was generally used, it proved particularly suitable for the hours of candlelight when other forms of work might have to be laid aside. Mrs Delany, after a visit to the Court in 1782, recorded that Queen Charlotte 'was making a fringe, in a frame, and did me the honour to show me how to do it and to say that she thought it was a work that would not try my eyes'.

When plaiting braids, for which longer lengths of yarn were needed, it was found convenient to wind each thread on to a short bobbin, and it is for this purpose that the bone or ivory fish sometimes found in an old work-box were used. They closely resemble the fish counters that were needed in quantity at this period for playing quadrille and other card games, but may be distinguished by their more rounded form and the elongated tail, necessary to provide room for winding on the thread (Plate 180). They were later supplanted by small wooden bobbins shaped at both ends in such a manner that they could be mounted and filled on an ordinary sewing machine.

Towards the end of the Victorian era macramé work enjoyed a renewed popularity. Deep tasselled borders, made from thread sold specially for this purpose, were tacked to the edges of mantelpieces, shelves and corner brackets, and became a conspicuous feature of late 19th-century furnishing (Plate 181). Meanwhile, the fish bobbins, now outmoded, had been finding their way into boxes of old card counters where, among their slimmer companions, a new use had been found for them, and where, in fact, many of them still remain to this day.

In comparatively early times it was realised that this method of twisting thread had its limitations: the close knotting by its very nature tended to make the work stiff and unyielding and it was therefore quite unsuited for the decoration of fine materials, the folds of which demanded a softer, more pliable trimming. Moreover, when making a narrow border or insertion, the constant knotting of short threads into a horizontal heading was extremely tedious. Eventually it was discovered that these difficulties could be overcome if the strip of trimming, instead of being worked horizontally, from left to right, was worked vertically on the pillow in the same way as when making braids, the threads now running through the length instead of the width of the strip (Plate 189).

These threads, which might be many yards long, were wound on to bobbins and, the loose ends having been attached to pins stuck into the pillow, were spread out to hang down in front of the worker. Knotting had been dispensed with: patterns were formed entirely by twisting or plaiting, so that where the finest thread was employed trimmings of the utmost softness and delicacy could be made. It was in this manner that lace-making, as we understand the term today, evolved.

For bobbins, the early lace-workers used bones, probably sheep's trotters, so that the work became known as bone lace: Shakespeare, in *Twelfth Night*, refers to 'the free maids who weave their thread with bones'. When, in time, wooden bobbins came to be used, the term pillow lace was adopted, though coarse work, for which a thicker thread was employed, was sometimes referred to as bobbin lace. The designs followed, unlike those of knotted-thread work and the early reticella laces, which were of necessity formal and geometrical, could be as free-flowing as was desired. The pattern was first drawn on a strip of parchment or card and pricked over at close intervals along the curving lines and at all points where the threads were to cross; this strip was then fixed to the pillow immediately underneath the threads (Plate 182).

The holes received the pins which were stuck firmly into the pillow to control the stitches and hold them in position, those at the back being moved forward and used again in the front as the pattern progressed, while the worker, with palms held downwards, crossed and re-crossed the threads, tossing the bobbins backwards and forwards with the tips of the fingers. As in former centuries metal pins were expensive, and liable through rust to stain the threads, the early lace-makers whittled down fish or chicken bones to serve the same purpose. For a simple edging there would be about sixty threads to be held in position; for a wide flounce there might be five or six hundred.

So far as can be ascertained the plaiting and weaving of fine lace was becoming established in this country in the third quarter of the 16th century, at which time it appears to have been well known in Saxony and also in Italy and Spain. In the county of Bedfordshire it has been claimed that it was first taught in England by Katherine of Aragon, wife of Henry VIII, when she was residing at Ampthill from 1531 to 1533, but there is no definite proof of its having been developed here at so early a date. What is more probable is that, as Katherine and many of her ladies were accomplished needlewomen, they introduced to the village the fashion for white work that was at that time sweeping across Europe, more particularly the art of making trimmings and insertions, and that, in consequence, Ampthill early acquired an interest in, and reputation for, work of this type.

Although so little is known of its early history there can be no doubt that the development of pillow lace in this country was greatly influenced by the influx of lace-workers from the Continent in the latter part of the 16th century.

It was no mere matter of chance that the industry became established in the eastern half of England. Fleeing from religious persecution in their own countries, these refugees from the Netherlands and France landed on the east coast and made their way to the counties of Bedford, Buckingham and Northampton, as well as to Honiton in Devon where, most probably, braids or 'laces' were already being made. Here they set up their pillows and began to earn a meagre livelihood for themselves by plaiting and twisting the fine laces for which they were renowned in their homeland, introducing new patterns and techniques to the native inhabitants of the villages in which they had come to live.

After the Revocation of the Edict of Nantes in 1685 there was a large influx of refugees and the lace-making industry spread gradually to other counties, notably to Oxfordshire, Somerset and Wiltshire, the type and pattern of the work in each county corresponding in most cases with that of the town or district on the Continent from which the workers had fled. The Honiton lace-makers, for instance, adopted the patterns and methods of the Brussels workers, while those in the East Midlands followed the techniques employed in Mechlin, Lille and Valenciennes.

The tools and accessories used in lace-making vary considerably in different countries and regions, not solely as a matter of tradition but according to the type of lace being made. In the English Midlands pillows are usually square with rounded corners (Plate 187). In Italy they are often muff-shaped; in this latter case the pricked pattern is placed round the pillow which can be revolved as the work proceeds so that the lace is worked on a continuous parchment strip. Similar muff-shaped cushions are used in Germany and Russia. A more elaborate type of cushion, used on the Continent when a narrow lace is being made, has a small, revolving cylinder built in towards the back, on to which the lengthening strip can be wound.

For the Brussels and Honiton laces, where constant turning in different directions is necessary, a much flatter pillow is generally used. In Belgium it may be mushroom shaped, in the form of a padded board revolving on a pivot mounted on top of a box, with a drawer in it for holding pins and other accessories; here the flatness of the pillow provides support for the bobbins and prevents any undue strain being put on the fine threads. In complete contrast, in Spanish and Maltese lace-making, where tension is of great importance, the bobbins hang down from long, bolster-shaped pillows propped on tall, adjustable stands, the parchment being placed lengthwise, from top to bottom (Plate 186).

Pillow stands, though varying in type, are common to all countries and were formerly of great importance as they enabled the lace-makers to bring their work out into the daylight in fine weather, the dimly lit interiors of most old cottages being quite unsuitable for setting out an intricate pattern or plaiting fine threads. In this country a wooden stand is usually known as a pillow-horse, or sometimes as a 'maid' or 'lady'; it may be three or four legged, square or round topped, or merely some simple folding device against which the worker could prop her pillow when resting it on her lap.

As the type of pillow used varied in different districts, so the shape and size of the bobbins varied with the different kinds of lace. Here tradition played a much stronger part, each locality developing distinctive styles and patterns, which has given these small implements a charm and individuality of their own and has made them of great interest to collectors. Most bobbins are composed of a long shank surmounted by a narrow neck on to which the thread is wound; on the top of this there is often a further, shorter neck round which the end of the thread is taken in a half-hitch to secure it, but enabling it to be unwound gradually, with a slight pull, as the work proceeds. Wood and bone are the materials commonly used, but ivory was also employed, and metal and glass very occasionally.

For the Lille, Valenciennes and Maltese laces, where tension was of great importance, the bobbins were made of a heavy wood, while the base of the shank might also be bulbous to give additional weight. On the other hand, for Brussels or Honiton lace, where a very delicate thread is used, the bobbins, or lace sticks as they are termed, must be extremely light. The shank must also be slim and pointed at the base, as, in the 'sewings', that is, the joining of the separate sprigs and sprays to the fine, net-like background, a type of work for which the locality is famous, the bobbins must themselves pass through certain portions of the lace. Their slender form allows for little variation in shape, but they are often decorated with a characteristic, incised black and red check patterning, and with initials, crosses, hearts and motifs connected with the sea. A typical Honiton lace-stick is illustrated on the extreme right of the top row of Plate 189, but there is also a blunt ended bobbin with a double neck that was used for making Devon Trolley lace.

In the counties of the East Midlands where tension was of primary concern, the lace-workers found their own solution to the problem of weight. They fashioned their bobbins from straight pieces of wood, bone or ivory, attaching to the base a loop of copper wire strung with coloured beads (Plates 189 and 190). This decoration was known as a spangle; apart from providing the necessary pull on the threads, it had the added advantage of holding the bobbin steady against the pillow. Of the nine beads of which many old spangles are composed there are often three on each side, of tinted glass, known as 'square-cuts', with indentations formed in the making by pressing the semi-molten metal between two files. At the bottom is the odd bead, larger, and perhaps multi-coloured, or of amber, coral or cornelian.

Instruction in lace-making began at an early age; many children attended the village lace-schools where they sat chanting the traditional songs or 'tells', similar to the old knitting songs, each verse changing with the alterations of the pattern as the work proceeded. To a young girl a large bead for a lace bobbin might be a treasured possession, a gift, probably from an admirer or sweetheart; it might even be replaced by a button, a coin or other small trinket.

Not only did the Midland workers attach spangles to their bobbins, they began to ornament them in other ways. Those made of bone or ivory could be stained in bright colours; some were decorated with spiral grooves turned in a lathe and wound with silver or brass wire; others were inlaid with pewter spots and bands and were known familiarly as 'Leopards' and 'Tigers'. 'Butterfly' bobbins have pewter decoration, in relief, in the shape of insects' wings. 'Tallies' have a broad band of tin or pewter round the shank, enabling the worker to recognise them easily; they were used in Buckinghamshire for working the 'plaits' or dots with which the net ground was sprinkled. In Bedfordshire, when a coarse thread was needed for outlining a pattern, stout, wooden 'Trailer' or 'Trolley' bobbins were used, weighted with loose pewter rings called gingles. Very different in character are the delicate 'Bitted' bobbins inlaid with thin strips of coloured woods, more decorative, perhaps, than practical, as so few have survived intact after the wear and tear of years.

On bone and ivory bobbins names of both men and women are frequently found; the letters are formed by a series of indentations pricked or drilled on one side, or spirally, along the bobbin and filled in afterwards with blue, black or red paint (Plate 191). It is likely that many of these were made and given as love-tokens, but they could also be bought from pedlars and at village fairs, and from recognised bobbin-makers; in some examples the distinctive style of a particular craftsman is easily distinguishable. On commemorative bobbins, in addition to the date of a birth, marriage or death, the name of a town or village may be added. Phrases such as 'Don't tell Mother', 'Name the Day', 'Kiss me quick' and 'Love me or leave me' were extremely popular, the bobbins in some instances being given as presents on St Valentine's day, while for the more serious-minded 'God is love' and other religious sentiments were provided.

There were also cryptic or puzzle bobbins where the words had to be carefully deciphered; bobbins with political slogans, popular at election times; and historical or topical bobbins, recording notable events. A young man anxious to exhibit his skill in carving might fashion for himself, or as a gift, a 'Church-window' bobbin of wood or bone, with elongated openings and hollowed out in the centre. Similar in appearance, but even more intricate was the 'Mother-in-babe' bobbin, still much sought after by collectors, which contains in each of its hollowed out compartments a miniature bobbin about a quarter of an inch in length (Plate 190). A variation of this was the 'Bird-cage', where the open compartment contained miniature bobbins or coloured beads held in place by smaller beads threaded on fine wire.

'Jack-in-a-box' bobbins were made in two sections that when pulled apart revealed a tiny bobbin concealed inside; yet another type of bobbin made in two separate parts, used particularly for the manufacture of gold and silver lace, has a sheath or protector that could be slipped over the thread to prevent it from coming into contact with the hands.

A well-filled pincushion was a valuable asset in the making of pillow lace. It was also of great help to the lace-workers, when following a design, to have a number of pins different in appearance from the rest that would enable them to see at a glance what portion of the pattern had been reached. They were therefore in the habit of ornamenting some of their pins by threading on to them several small beads, fixed in place by a turn of wire; the hard round seeds of the Corn Goose-grass were used in a similar manner to form a distinctive head; alternatively, the top of the pin might be covered with a knob of sealing wax. In more recent days those who could afford them used coloured glass-headed pins.

Towards the bottom of the lace-maker's pincushion in Plate 192, it will be noticed, there is a pin with a glass head shaped in the form of a heart—probably a Valentine gift. Prickers, for marking out the pattern, sometimes had heart-shaped heads of bone, perhaps with the initials of the recipient or donor. In Honiton a similar, sharp-pointed implement, set in a wooden handle and known as a needlepin, was used in joining the separate motifs to the delicate background (Plate 189).

Though the making of fine pillow lace was developed in the West (the clothing of the Oriental peoples being unsuited to decoration of this kind), the art has from time to time been introduced into Eastern countries, more especially by European missionaries. In these circumstances the bobbins were made by native craftsmen, often of ivory with elaborate and skilful carving, and, though difficult to classify, are readily distinguishable from the more homely, simply-made implements of this country or the Continent.

Sets of carved ivory bobbins were sometimes made to the order of Europeans resident in India and neighbouring regions, to be sent home as presents to relatives and friends, but they are by no means common; for whereas a tambour frame could grace a drawing room, and a distaff and spindle might be found at Court, few women of note concerned themselves with the plaiting of the fine collars, cuffs, flounces and insertions with which their dresses were so liberally trimmed. Throughout its history the lace pillow has been associated with poverty.

For filling the neck of a lace bobbin with thread a specially devised winder was used. A typical example may be seen in Plate 193, mounted on a stand with a drawer beneath for holding accessories. The rim of the large wheel is grooved and has a short handle; when turned, it revolves the hollow bobbin-holder on the left, to which it is geared by means of a cord. On to the upright peg at the end of the long arm a skein holder is slipped; this is composed of two flat blades of wood known as yarningles, placed over one another to form a cross, with a series of holes at the extremities into which short pegs could be inserted to take skeins of different lengths. The end of the thread having been attached to the neck of the bobbin, the base, with the spangle, was wound round with a piece of cloth or soft paper so that it might be held firmly when pushed into the cup-shaped holder. The worker then turned the wheel with her right hand, and with the fingers of the left hand steadied the bobbin while guiding the thread backwards and forwards.

In this instance the long arm for supporting the yarningles, attached loosely by a screw, swivels round to lie at the back of the wheel when not in use; but with some winders, particularly those that clamp on to a table, an entirely separate skein holder must be used. Where no spangles are involved, winders may have spring clips, to grip the bobbin, in place of the cup-shaped holder.

A number of implements used by lace-makers in the Midland counties may be seen in Plate 187. On the left is one of the large glass bottles that were filled with water and placed by the workers in front of a candle to serve as a condensing lens; to the right of this is a smaller flask or 'flash', stoppered and inverted, and fitting in a wooden stand. In the centre is a tall candle-block or flash-stool with inverted flashes, set in wooden sockets ranged round it, thus enabling several persons to work by the light of a single candle fixed in an adjustable holder in the middle. Three rush baskets or 'hutches' used for carrying the glass bottles are hanging in the background; on the ground is a bobbin-winder and two boxes for spare bobbins and thread.

Examples of such implements, which differ considerably in detail in each of the lace-making districts, are on view in several local museums in this country. Luton Museum and Art Gallery, in Bedfordshire, has a comprehensive display of tools and accessories, including a particularly fine collection of lace bobbins.[1]

[1] See also *The Romance of the Lace Pillow*, T. Wright, Olney, 1919, 2nd edition, 1924; *Pillow Lace in the East Midlands*, C. Freeman, 1960, Luton Museum, Wardown Park, Luton, Bedfordshire; and *Toys and Tools of Stitchery*, G. Whiting, 1928, Columbia University Press, U.S.A.

15

Patterns and Pattern Books

IT WAS NOT until the beginning of the 16th century, more than fifty years after the invention of printing, that publishers began to turn their attention to printing books of patterns for use in needlework. Before this time designs had been handed down as a matter of tradition from one generation to the next. Children, watching or helping their elders, became familiar at an early age with certain arrangements of colours and stitches and soon learned to reproduce them from memory. Patterns were associated, not only with particular regions, but with particular families. In many households examples of stitches and designs were worked, in a long strip, to be preserved carefully for future generations. With the advent of printing these pattern strips lost their former importance, as knowledge was now more widely diffused, and designs spread from village to village and from country to country. The original purpose of the sampler was thus largely forgotten and it became an educational exercise for children, or an object of decoration to hang on a wall—a proof of the embroiderer's skill rather than a record of designs.

The earliest known printed pattern books for needlework were published in Germany in the early 1520s, the most notable, probably, that of Peter Quentel published at Cologne in 1527. As might be expected in that country, many of the designs were suitable for knitting, but they could also be used for weaving and other forms of work. A few years later a number of elegant parchment covered booklets with patterns for embroidery, and a frontispiece depicting the various tools and accessories used in weaving, stitching and bobbin work, were published in Italy. Their circulation was extremely limited as they were costly to produce and, at first, they were little known outside the exclusive coterie of queens, princesses and other ladies of noble rank, to whom they were dedicated.

The designs, delicately printed on thin, opaque paper, were often commissioned from artists of repute who might afterwards reproduce some of the finished embroideries in their paintings. It was with the aid of these booklets, the titles of which were as flowery and extravagant as the language of their long prefaces extolling the virtues of their patrons, that the great ladies of Venice and their daughters decorated their clothing and household linen, and worked fine vestments and furnishings for the use of the Church.

Few have survived into modern times; most are in poor repair, their pages worn with constant usage and the patterns pricked through and smeared with pounce. Early examples, such as those of Zoppino and Vavassore published in 1532, gave directions for cross-stitch, drawn and counted thread work, Holbein and satin stitch, and embroidery on net; but after the middle of the century cut-work and lace were their main concern. Mathio Pagan's *La Gloria et l'honore dei ponti tagliati* appeared in 1558, and when this was followed some years later by Cesare Vecellio's *Corona delle nobili e virtuose donne* with its delicate designs for *punto in aria*, it became obvious that it was this new and more fanciful form of work that was to captivate the people of Italy.

Translations of these books soon reached other parts of Europe, and by the beginning of the 17th century Federico Vinciolo's famous designs for lacis and embroidery were as well known in Paris and London as they were in Venice.

There were at the same time books intended for the use of wood-carvers, metalworkers and craftsmen in general, such as Alciat's *Emblems*, first published in Milan in 1522, and Whitney's *A Choice of Emblemes*, printed more than fifty years later in Leyden, from which designs for embroidery could be taken. The pattern used in making a delicate lace ruffle might equally well be found damascened on to a sword blade or a suit of armour. With the further development of printing more specialised books became available, of which the best known in this country are Shorleyker's *A Schole-house for the Needle* (1624), and Boler's *The Needle's Excellency* that had reached several editions by 1630. This last volume contains the now famous poem, *The Prayse of the Needle*, with its long catalogue of stitches, by John Taylor, the water-poet.

Stuart designers turned to the herbals and bestiaries of the period. Dr Thomas Muffett's *Insectorum, sive minimorum Animalium Theatrum*, published posthumously in London in 1634, and translated into English in 1658, proved a rich source of new ideas, though surely nobody would have been more astonished than its learned author to find that it had inspired the needlewomen of the next half-century to decorate their embroideries with representations o snails, flies, caterpillars and beetles. By Charles II's reign sheets of engravings, taken from natural history and other works, were being printed specially for the use of embroiderers.

In the Orient, books intended for a similar purpose were also making their appearance. The Japanese encyclopaedias of design, with their many hundreds of patterns (Plate 194), could have provided ample material for Western embroiderers, but seem to have attracted little attention in Europe, though Stalker and Parker's *Treatise of Japaning and Varnishing* (1688) had brought with it a vogue for *chinoiseries*, its patterns being widely copied by designers in many other crafts, including embroidery.

For those who could afford them, materials could be bought with patterns drawn, or occasionally printed from wood blocks, ready for working. Before the middle of the 18th century tradesmen specialising in the colouring of maps were employing large numbers of men and women to draw and paint designs on linen, silk and velvet, and it was they, no doubt, who introduced the fashion for map embroidery, thus paving the way for the map sampler, a combined exercise in geography and stitchery that became general in the schoolrooms of the late Georgian period. Copies of prints and well-known paintings were also made for embroidery. An interesting example of the varied treatment afforded to the same picture by different designers is to be found in Plates 195 and 196, both of which are painted on silk. Where the background was composed of felt, faces and hands painted and cut from paper were supplied with the material.

The ladies' magazines of the period, mainly literary in character, seldom concerned themselves with needlework, for this was the age of the blue-stocking who had neither the inclination nor the training to cope with complicated instructions in embroidery. Periodicals devoted to fashions and romantic stories might occasionally introduce a supplement with patterns for needle-work, or a page entitled 'The Work-table', but it is obvious that they were catering for a minority of their readers. There are, nevertheless, some delightful little pattern folders to be found in work-boxes of the late 18th and early 19th centuries. Seldom more than a few inches square, they pull out to disclose twenty or thirty designs, in minute black-and-white checks, of a date much older than the folders themselves, including many examples of lettering and numerals, in addition to patterns suitable for knitting, net-work and canvas embroidery in wool, silk and beads (Plate 197).

During the latter half of the 18th century the pictures executed in woolwork by Miss Eliza Morritt, Mrs Knowles and Miss Mary Linwood had been attracting much attention in the fashionable world; many of them were reproductions of portraits by famous artists. To copy a large portrait in wool was no mean achievement. Even where the picture was first outlined or painted on the material, every detail of the original, in the many different shades, had to be followed with meticulous care, stitch by stitch, a process requiring so much skill and patient application that it was unlikely to have attracted any but the most dedicated needlewomen.

In the year 1804, however, it occurred to a German print seller, named Phillipson, who had close connections with this country, that woolwork of this kind could be greatly popularised if, with the use of fine copper plates, he was to print sheets of paper so that they were covered all over with a network of small squares on which patterns could be painted by hand in colour. It would then no longer be necessary to outline or paint the picture on to the material: the embroiderer could work from the hand-coloured print, as each square would represent one short stitch. With the fine and closely woven canvas of the period, this involved much counting of threads, but by the introduction of vertical stripes into the canvas, by making every tenth thread of the warp a coloured thread, the process was considerably eased. Finally, about 1825, the work was made extremely simple by the production of a double thread canvas, similar to that in use today, the material to be embroidered now consisting of a network of squares corresponding to those of the printed pattern.

Phillipson's invention, which was to influence the fashion in needlework in this country for more than half a century, did not at the time attract much attention, and it was eventually an embroidress, Frau Wittich, the wife of a Berlin print seller, who, seeing the possibilities of such an enterprise, persuaded her husband to commercialise this method of pattern-making on a large scale. In 1810 Wittich began by producing patterns for footstools and cushions, some of them from his wife's original designs. By means of letters or symbols, he indicated what paints were required. The patterns were passed along a row of workers each of whom quickly filled in, with a small square-tipped brush of the same width as the printed squares, that part of the design that was of the particular shade allotted to them. The finished patterns were priced at two or three shillings each (Plate 198).

G. E. Falbe was another early print seller whose designs were exported to this country, literally in their thousands, the exact materials for working them being supplied at the same time. Shops specialising in needlework often advertised that they were 'importers direct of new Berlin patterns, with canvas and crewels of the correct shades'. There was soon a demand for larger and more ambitious designs, and artists were engaged to make squared copies of well-known pictures. Landseer's famous painting of Bolton Abbey prepared in this manner for copying cost more than £40. Portraits of royalty were extremely popular. The ladies of Mrs Gaskell's *Cranford* are described as being occupied with the new 'Loyal woolwork', but Miss Matty, who had 'once been able to trace out patterns very nicely for muslin embroidery, by dint of placing a piece of silver-paper over the design to be copied, and holding both against the window-pane while she marked the scallop and eyelet-holes', was suffering from failing eyesight. It was doubted 'if she could discover the number of threads in a worsted-work pattern, or rightly appreciate the different shades required for Queen Adelaide's face.'

Berlin patterns, unlike earlier designs for needlework, were not marred by pricking or pouncing and, being painted on stout paper, could withstand reasonable wear and tear. In good condition they are an interesting side-line for the collector who will soon recognise the subdued tones of the early years of the century; the brilliant hues of the roses, violets, petunias and convolvulus, introduced by such firms as Hertz and Wegener, when the work was in its hey-day; and the dark backgrounds and bilious greens and yellows of the acorns and oak leaves that characterised a later phase. By the middle of Queen Victoria's reign hand painting had been replaced by colour printing, designs had deteriorated and the work had lost much of its earlier charm; indeed, the greatest recommendation for any form of needlework at this time was that 'no special skill or previous experience is necessary'.

The period is, nevertheless, not without its importance in the long history of needlework. By the early 1880s Thérèse de Dillmont, of Dornach, Alsace, was already compiling her *Ouvrages des Dames*, which we know in this country as the *Encyclopaedia of Needlework*, a publication that was to raise the standard of technique and design in almost all branches of sewing and embroidery. Translated into several languages, it is as remarkable today as it was at the time of its first appearance, and still remains a reliable text-book and a valuable source of reference.

The Practice of Parfilage

PARFILAGE, or drizzling as it was called in this country, was a curious occupation that first came into vogue at the luxurious Court of Versailles during the reign of Louis XVI. It consisted of picking out or unravelling the gold and silver threads of laces, braids, tassels and embroideries from outworn coats, dresses, uniforms and furnishings for the purpose of reselling them to a goldsmith, who melted them down and recovered the precious metal. Its connection with needlework, of which it is the exact opposite, may seem to be remote; but as it involved the use of sewing implements it has an association with many of the subjects dealt with in this book. From France in the late 18th century the practice of parfilage spread to Austria where, for a time, it became so popular a pastime in Court circles that it ousted most other forms of feminine amusement. Lady Mary Coke, in a letter describing the life of the Austrian Court at this period, says: 'All the ladies who do not play at cards pick gold. 'Tis the most general fashion I ever saw.'

The practice of returning costly gold and silver trimmings to the tradesman who originally supplied them was not in itself new. Household bills of the 17th and 18th centuries show that it was customary for the silvermen and lacemen, from whom such goods were bought, to take back any lace left over, or to re-buy the old lace after it had been removed from worn coats and dresses. Peter Bunnell, laceman of the Golden Cock in Bedford Street, who in 1757 sold, for the use of the Duke of Bedford, twenty-two yards of rich gold brocade and scolloped lace at eighteen shillings a yard, advertised on his bill that he gave full value for all gold lace returned; thus, incidentally, ensuring to the customer the quality of the material supplied. The exact weight of the lace sold was carefully recorded on the bill at the time of sale.[1]

The unravelling of gold and silver thread as a socially accepted pastime was something quite different. Those who indulged in it were known as *parfileuses*. They carried with them, in their pockets, small embroidered

[1] From *The Russells in Bloomsbury, 1669–1771*, by Gladys Scott Thompson. Cape, 1940.

pouches or *sacs* containing the necessary tools—a pointed implement, such as a stiletto, for unpicking the thread; a pair of scissors; and a knife for cutting the stitches of the couching. The tools were taken to all parties and social functions, and even to the theatre, for it was on such occasions that most of the unpicking was done. As the fashion grew, sets of implements specially made for use in parfilage became obtainable, contained in richly decorated cases. These sets of tools are now extremely rare, though it is possible that some may still exist that remain unrecognised. The example in Plate 199, with its case of silver and blue enamel, was designed to be worn at the waist suspended by a cord. The scissors fit into the main body of the case; the unpicking tool, sometimes called a drizzling pin, and the thread knife, slip into sheaths on either side.

Although as a pastime parfilage was innocent enough at its inception, in the surroundings of the French Court it soon developed into a craze; for, as might be imagined, in the extravagant days of Marie Antoinette, those who indulged in it were inspired not so much by thrift as by an overwhelming desire for gain. Many of the more enthusiastic devotees of the practice did not hesitate openly to ask the gentlemen of their acquaintance for old epaulettes, laces and sword knots, and took a pleasure in vying with one another as to the amount they could obtain. Indeed, it soon became customary for them to take with them to social functions, and even to court, huge picking bags into which they put the gifts collected from their admirers. According to one 18th-century writer, 'a bold and beautiful *parfileuse* might make over 100 Louis-d'or a year by this industry'.

So insatiable was the craving of the ladies of the Court for material to put in their picking bags that the goldsmiths of the period began to manufacture small objects wound over with gold or silver thread which were sold as presents for unravelling. In place of the more customary gifts of flowers, perfumes and diamonds, a fashionable beau would give to the lady of his choice on New Year's Day a few dozen gold tassels or a length of gold lace. Madame de Genlis, recounting her experiences at the French court, says in her *Mémoires*: 'I have seen the Maréchale de Luxembourg give Madame de Blot a muslin apron trimmed with gold fringe and put up in a packet containing, besides its own value, about fifteen or twenty louis' worth of fringes. I have seen Madame de Boufflers receive from the Duke of Lauzun an imitation harp made of gold fringe which cost nearly a thousand francs. All this was untwisted to be sold at half price.'

Madame de Genlis also relates that on one occasion, at Chantilly, she wagered twenty-four gold bobbins of 12 francs each with the Duke of Coigny

149. An embroiderer's workroom in the 18th century. The woman on the left is holding up a large adjustable frame with one side of a coat outlined on the material ready for embroidery.

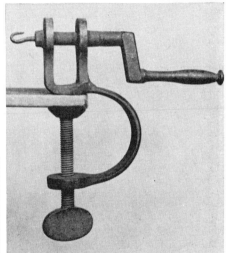

150. (Above) Iron clamp for making a twisted cord; 17th century.

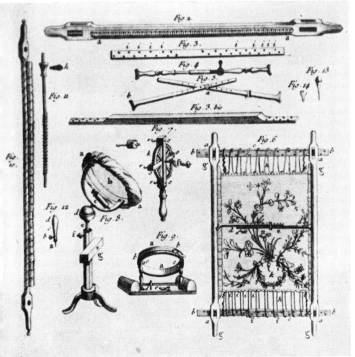

151. Old print showing parts of an adjustable embroidery frame, and frame completed. In the centre is a cord-making wheel, and below tambour frames of two different types; 18th century.

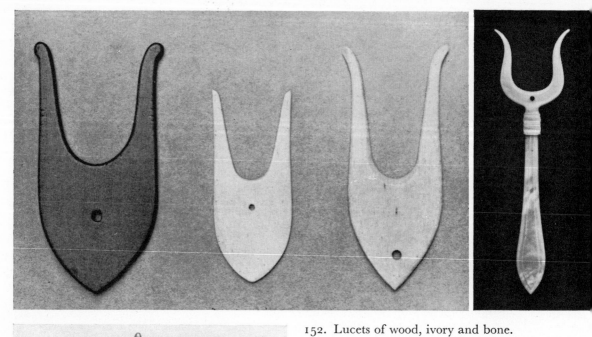

152. Lucets of wood, ivory and bone.
153. Long-handled mother-of-pearl lucet.

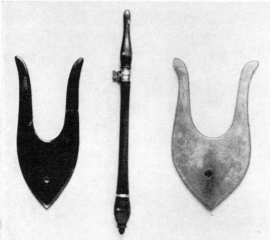

154. Lucets of tortoiseshell and horn. (*centre*)
Gold mounted ivory tambour hook stained to
imitate tortoiseshell.

155. (*above*) Fringing-fork, and small fork for
use in hairpin-work. (*below*) Two lucets and an
ebony tube for cord-making.

156. *Mme Antoine Crozat, Marquise du Châtel*, by J. A. J. Aved, 1741. The embroidery frame, shown in a horizontal position, is typical of the period. It could be pivoted and secured by a locking device seen on the extreme left. A shallow basket with silks, etc., is on the right.

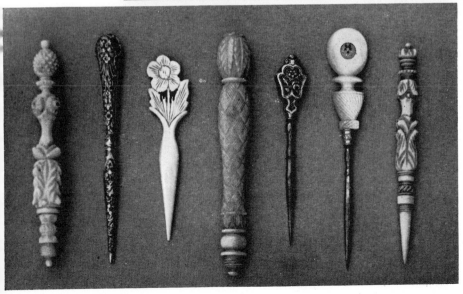

157. Stilettos with ornamental handles of ivory, silver and mother-of-pearl. In the first and fourth the point, which is reversible, is screwed upwards into the handle; the second has a detachable sheath.

158. *La Mère Laborieuse*, by Chardin (1699–1779). The woman seated is tambouring, the thread running direct from the revolving skein holder.

159. *The Ladies Waldegrave*, by Sir Joshua Reynolds (1723–1792). One is tambouring; the other two are winding silk thread on to a card.

160. Tambour frame on wooden stand, with reel beneath; from an 18th-century print.

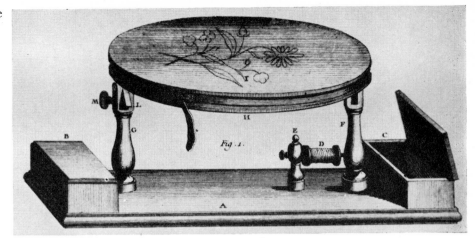

161. Silver spool-knave with ivory reel, worn when tambouring; Dutch, 1809.

162. Reel holder or spool-knave, of steel, for tambouring; 18th century.

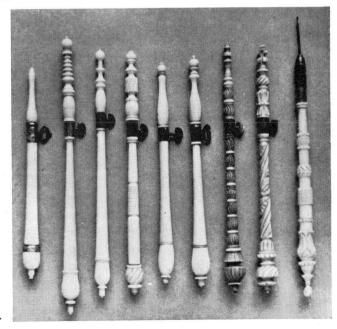

163. Turned ivory tambour hooks; the point protectors unscrew and there are spare hooks contained in the hollow handles.

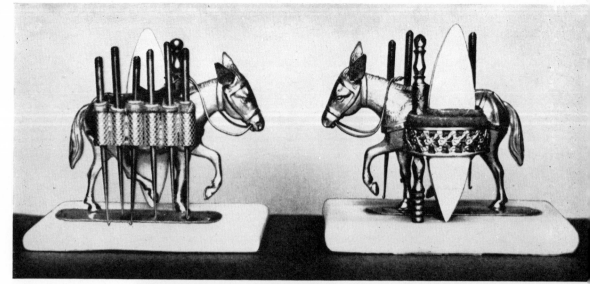

164. Gilded metal donkeys on alabaster bases, with panniers containing ivory tatting shuttles and sets of crochet hooks; Spanish, c. 1800.

165. (Above) Victorian crochet hook cases.

166. Steel implements for hairpin crochet, showing method of working.

67. Doyley with centre of ordinary crochet
nd edging of hairpin crochet.

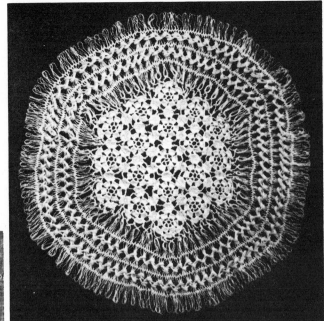

168. Muslin apron with tambour embroidery; the
centres of the flowers are worked with a needle. The
'invisible mending' is typical of the period (*see* Plate 17).

69. Doyley with edging of hairpin crochet.

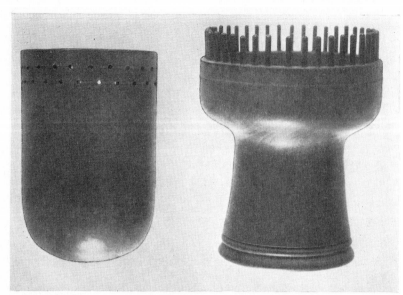

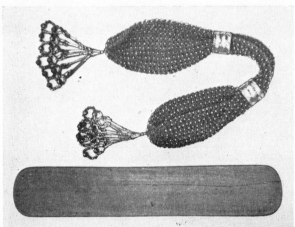

170. Wooden thimble-shaped purse mould;
17th or early 18th century. (*right*) Wooden purse
mould with pegs, sometimes known as a
Moule Turc.

171. Silk purse, having a beaded crochet top
and a base of bead crochet to take the wear of
the coins; early 19th century.

172. Wallet purse of beaded crochet, with the
wooden mould used in sewing up the seam
and ends.

173. Purse worked with beads, *à feston*, on a
thimble-shaped purse mould, *c.* 1800.

174. Knitted silk purse with base of fine bead-
knitting, and (*right*) ribbon purse woven over a
square mould; 18th century.

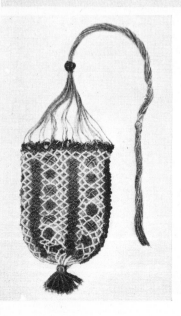

175. Purse with crochet silk top and base of bead knitting; early 19th century. 176. Girdle of bright coloured beads, a typical example of Indian beadwork. Handscreen of small glass beads made on an Apache loom; English, 18th century.

177. An Apache loom with partially completed beadwork.

178. *Viscountess Middleton, with a small table loom,* by Angelica Kauffmann (1741–1807).

179. Mahogany table loom; the initials E.D. are inlaid on the scroll-carved rail; English, 18th century.

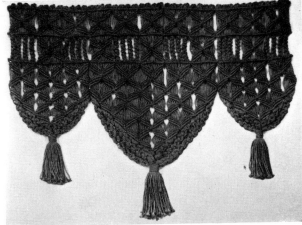

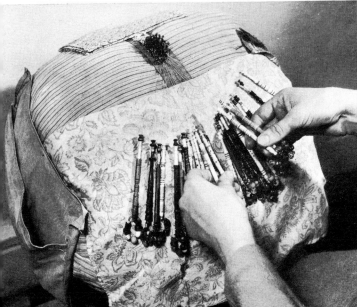

180. Bone bobbins for macramé work, one wound with thread.

181. Border of macramé work, the threads gathered in at the base to form tassels.

182. (Left) Cushion dressed for working, in Luton Museum, Bedfordshire. The bag for spare bobbins hangs on the left. The patterned cloth or 'worker' takes the friction of the bobbins and protects the parchment from becoming soiled. Another cloth, the 'drawter', covers the upper part of the parchment and keeps the finished lace clean.

83. Black Brussels or Chantilly order, 8″ in depth. This delicate pillow-lace cost 20 guineas a yard at the court of Marie Antoinette. After the Revolution it was made in Brussels by workers fleeing from France.

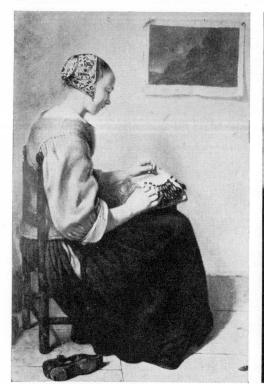

184. *The Lace-maker*, by C. Netscher (1639–1684).   185. *La Dentellière*, by Vermeer of Delft (1632-1675).
On the left is a cushion-shaped box, the forerunner of the modern work-box.

186. A Maltese lace-
maker. Here the lace
is worked down the
length of the pillow,
not around it.

187. Implements of the Lace
Industry in the English Midland
Counties.

188. Pillow-lace edgings
from the East Midlands.
Unlike the needle-made
laces, these were worked
vertically in a long strip,
the straight edge (or
engrêlure) always on the
right; the undulating,
outside edge (or couronne)
on the left.

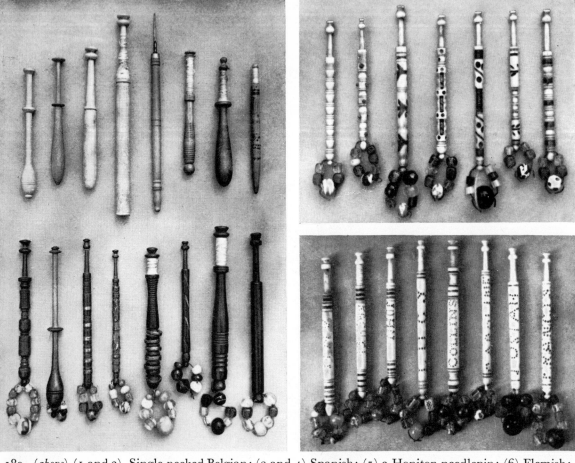

189. (*above*) (1 and 2), Single-necked Belgian; (3 and 4) Spanish; (5) a Honiton needlepin; (6) Flemish; (7) French; (8) Honiton; all are of wood. (*below*) Wooden bobbins from East Midlands: (1) turned, with typical spangle of 'square cuts' and centre-bead; (2) French origin, spangled in the East Midlands; (3) Bedfordshire Tiger; (4) Butterfly; (5) trolley with pewter gingles; (6) bitted; (7) trolley or coarse Torchon; (8) carved or whittled. 190. Midland bobbins of bone and ivory with pewter and painted decoration. In the centre is a 'mother-in-babe' bobbin. 191. Named bobbins of bone and ivory from the East Midlands.

192. (Below left) Lace-maker's pincushion decorated with gold thread and sequins, and stuck with metal and glass-headed pins.

193. (Above) Old bobbin winder, with drawer beneath for spare bobbins, etc. A pair of blades or yarningles, to hold the skein, were slipped over the spindle on the movable arm; the base of the bobbin was wound round with soft paper to hold it in the cup.

94. Pattern books, from Japanese En-
cyclopedias of Design; the smaller, one of
two volumes; the larger, one of four.

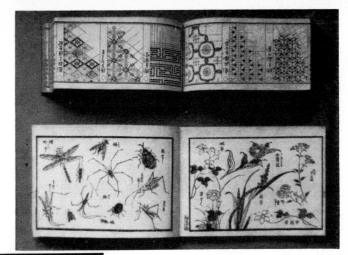

195. Reproduction of a picture repre-
senting *The Finding of Moses*, painted
on silk and embroidered.

196. Reproduction of the same picture,
by a different copyist, painted on silk and
embroidered with figures in costumes of
the 1790s.

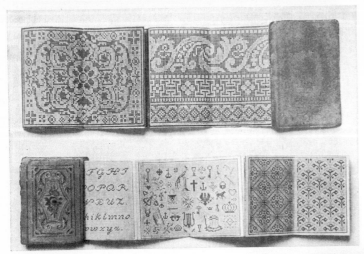

197. Pattern folder, $2\frac{1}{2}'' \times 3\frac{1}{2}''$, with 20 elaborate designs for lacis or canvas work; English, late 18th century. (*below*) Child's pattern folder opening to 60″ in length and with 11 different alphabets; German, *c.* 1820.

198. An early pattern for Berlin Woolwork, published by L. W. Wittich. The squared background is from a copper-plate engraving, the design is hand painted.

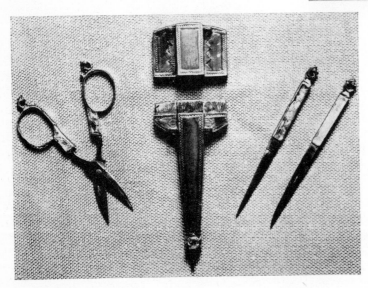

199. Set of tools for parfilage or drizzling; the case, of silver and blue enamel, has four suspension rings for cord to hang from the waist. The unpicking tool and thread knife fit into sheaths on either side of the scissor case; French, 18th century.

that she would mount one of the cascades like a staircase without falling. She won her bet and, having no interest herself in parfilage, divided the bobbins that evening among the ladies in the drawing room, who received them with delight, though they had affected to be greatly shocked at her escapade.

It was eventually as the result of Madame de Genlis's outspoken comments, and in particular her introduction of the following story into her novel, *Adèle et Théodore*, published in 1782, that the fashion of unravelling came to an end in France:

'One day before the promenade,' she writes, 'we were all assembled in the salon, when Madame de R—— remarks that the trimmings of gold of my coat would be excellent for unravelling. At the very instant a movement of gaiety compelled her to cut one of my fringes; immediately I was surrounded by ten women who, with a grace and a charming vivacity, undressed me, snatching away my coat and putting all my trimmings in their bags.'

This incident, as Madame de Genlis later explains, was inspired by an adventure that actually befell the Duc de Chartres; it was witnessed at the time by more than fifty people. By giving publicity to the occurrence she made many enemies for herself among the *parfileuses*, but she also succeeded at last in arousing the indignation of French society to the scandal of unravelling as it was practised in Court circles. 'Gradually,' she says, 'the enormous sacks of untwisted gold disappeared and in their stead came embroidery and tapestry.'

Parfilage was not introduced into England until more than ten years after it had gone out of fashion in France, for it was not until the outbreak of the Revolution that many of the half-starving and penniless members of the French aristocracy fled to this country and turned to picking gold as a means of eking out a precarious existence. The practice soon spread and, under the name of drizzling or ravelling, it became a fashionable pastime. That it gained as great a hold in some quarters here as on the Continent may be gauged by the following announcement which appeared in the *Weekly Despatch* on Sunday, September 27th, 1801: 'A very extraordinary robbery took place on Monday night in the House of Lords. The whole of the gold lace, and all the ornaments of the throne, the King's Arms excepted, were stripped off and carried away.'

For the most part, however, drizzling in this country remained a domestic pastime. Many large houses had their drizzling bags and boxes into which the trimmings of outworn uniforms, servants' liveries and upholsteries were put, as a matter of course, in readiness for unravelling—a custom that sounds harmless enough, but out of which developed a disastrous fashion for unpicking embroideries of all kinds that lasted well into the Victorian era and occasioned the destruction of much old and valuable needlework.

For a more detailed account of parfilage as it was practised here we are indebted, curiously enough, to a German actress, Caroline Bauer, who came to England in 1829 as the prospective bride of Prince Leopold, the widowed consort of Princess Charlotte and, greatly to her astonishment, found her suitor, a Field Marshal of England and a candidate for the Greek crown, bending over an elegant tortoiseshell drizzling box, picking thread after thread out of dusty cast-off gold and silver galloons.

Prince Leopold's addiction to drizzling and the incessant 'tsrr, tsrr, tsrr' which, she states, accompanied the process seem, indeed, to have been among the most vivid of the memories she retained of the unhappy year she spent in England. All her efforts to entertain him with music or reading aloud were fruitless. 'How I hated Drizzling!' she wrote in her memoirs many years later. 'When I saw the Prince, followed by his groom with that awful Drizzling box, alight from his carriage at once I felt the approach of a yawning fit. And even to this day, after more than a generation, I feel my heart cramped by the same distressing tendency to yawn.'

Caroline Bauer further recalls that, during the year she was in this country, Prince Leopold gained by his drizzling enough money to buy a handsome silver soup tureen, which he solemnly presented to his young niece, Princess Victoria of Kent, on the occasion of her eleventh birthday. 'I am sure', she comments, 'that Queen Victoria reverently preserves to this day the soup tureen earned by drizzling as a love gift from her uncle King Leopold of Belgium.'

The lack of further reliable information with regard to the equipment of the *parfileuse* has led to many statements being made which are very wide of the truth. For many years, for instance, it has been asserted that in a portrait by Louis le Tocqué (Plate 140), Madame Danger is depicted in the act of unravelling an edging of gold lace surrounding a sachet, and winding the thread upon an ornamental shuttle. In fact, she is knotting thread, the poise of the hands being characteristic of this form of work, while on close inspection the knotted portion of the cord can be clearly seen below her left hand. The so-called sachet on her lap is the usual large knotting bag, the ribbons of which are slung over her arm. That a *parfileuse* should have wound the salvaged thread on to a valuable knotting shuttle is highly improbable; it would only have had to be unwound before sending it to the refiner, whose sole object was to recover the precious metal.

It has also been assumed that some mechanical device was used in unravelling and winding the threads. There is no evidence, however, of any accessories being employed or needed other than the large bag or box for holding the material to be unravelled, and a set of tools as already described. The incessant 'tsrr, tsrr, tsrr' that accompanied the occupation, and which so irritated Caroline Bauer, was probably the noise of the threads being torn apart. It is likely that from this ripping sound the onomatopoeic term 'drizzling' was derived.

One reason why so little is recorded about this pastime may be that, fascinating as it was, its practice was only possible in the limited circles where gold and silver trimmings were readily obtainable; it therefore never attracted the attention of the people in general. To regard it as being merely of trivial or passing interest would, nevertheless, be a mistake. Unravelling was in vogue for well over fifty years and heralded a fashion for destruction that was to have most unfortunate results. Mrs E. L. Lowes, in her *Chats on old Lace and Needlework*, recalls that, in her childhood, she was allowed to pick to pieces a Stewart needlework picture in order to retrieve the corals and seed-pearls, to make them into a necklace for her doll. The loss to posterity, in this half century, of priceless tapestries, embroideries and other forms of needlework, destroyed for pleasure, gain or mistaken ideas of thrift, is impossible to estimate.

Index

132

FLORISSANT VALLEY COMMUNITY COLLEGE
ST. LOUIS, MO.

INVENTORY 1983

LIBRARY
FLORISSANT VALLEY COMMUNITY COLLEGE
ST. LOUIS, MO.